第二版　　同步翻譯權威　郭岱宗 著

同步翻譯實例

同步翻譯 **4**

東華書局

國家圖書館出版品預行編目資料

同步翻譯實例 / 郭岱宗著 . -- 二版 . -- 臺北市：臺灣東華，

民 101.05

520 面；17x23 公分

ISBN 978-957-483-706-9（平裝：附光碟）

1. 英國 2. 翻譯 3. 口譯

805.1   101008890

中華民國一〇一年五月二版

同步翻譯實例

定價　新臺幣伍佰伍拾元整

（外埠酌加運費匯費）

著　者　郭　　岱　　宗
發 行 人　卓　劉　慶　弟
出 版 者　臺灣東華書局股份有限公司
　　　　　臺北市重慶南路一段一四七號三樓
　　　　　電　話：(02)2311-4027
　　　　　傳　眞：(02)2311-6615
　　　　　郵　撥：00064813
　　　　　網　址：www.tunghua.com.tw
直營門市 1　臺北市重慶南路一段七十七號一樓
　　　　　電　話：(02)2371-9311
直營門市 2　臺北市重慶南路一段一四七號一樓
　　　　　電　話：(02)2382-1762

何謂上乘的口譯？

一切的翻譯理論，若是未能用於實際操作，都將淪為空談。

 口譯公式(The Formula of Interpretation)——郭岱宗

QI = EV + EK + FAAE

QI = Quality Interpreting（精於口譯）

EV = Encyclopedic Vocabulary（豐沛的字彙）

EK = Encyclopedic Knowledge（通達的見識）

F = **Fluency**（流暢）——

流暢的字彙	流暢的句子	敏捷的反應
流暢的記憶	流暢的思路	

A = **Accuracy**（準確）——

發音準確	腔調準確
文法準確	譯意準確

A = **Artistry**（藝術之美）——

文字之美	發音之美	台風之美
語調之美	聲音之美	

E = **Easiness**（輕鬆自在）

 金字塔理論
(The Pyramid Theory of Simultaneous Interpretation)——郭岱宗

「優質的同步口譯超越了點、線、面，它就像一座金字塔，由下而上，用了許多石塊，每一塊都是真材實料，紮紮實實地堆砌而成。」這些石塊包括了：

①深闊的字彙
②完整、優美、精確的譯文
③精簡俐落的句子
④迅速而正確的文法
⑤對雙文化貼切的掌握
⑥流暢的聽力
⑦字正腔圓
⑧優美愉悅的聲音
⑨適度的表情
⑩敏銳的聽眾分析和臨場反應
⑪穩健而親切的台風

最後，每一次口譯時，這些堆積的能量都隨點隨燃，立刻從金字塔的尖端爆發出來，這也就是最後一個石塊——快若子彈的速度！

這些石塊不但個個紮實，而且彼此緊密銜接、環環相扣，缺一不可，甚至不能鬆動。少了一角，或鬆了一塊，這個金字塔都難達高峰！

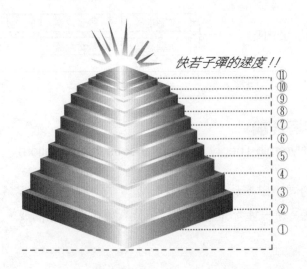

漣漪理論 (Ripple Theory) + **老鼠會方法**
(The Pyramid Scheme) **創造龐大且紮實的字彙庫** ──郭岱宗

字彙範圍須採用「漣漪方式」：

　　記背單字不應採用隨機或跳躍的方式，而應該像漣漪一樣，由近至遠，一圈一圈，緊密而廣闊。

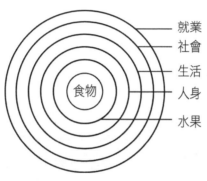

記背方法須用快速伸展字彙的「老鼠會方法」：

　　平日即必須累積息息相關、深具連貫性的字彙，口譯時才能快速、精確、輕鬆、揮灑自如！「由上而下」的「老鼠會式的字彙成長」，即以一個字為原點，發展為數個字，各個字又可繼續聯想出數個字。如此，一層層下來，將可快速衍生出龐大的字彙庫。既快速、有效、又不易忘。

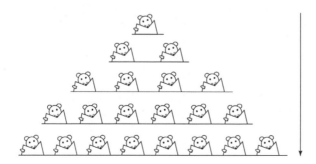

 ## Flower Theory 使我們的英語發聲圓潤優美——郭岱宗

中文因為受限於一、二、三、四聲的規範,所以有稜有角,使音域有限。英文則不同。我們以中文為母語的人,若要把英文說得優美、圓潤、高低自如,則可做以下想像:

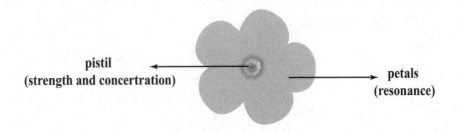

我們音質、音量、語調的製作,就像一朵花。中間花蕊 (pistil) 的部份是力量和精緻的音軸,旁邊綻放的花朵 (petals),則是共鳴、震動、擴散。pistil 不穩,則聲音不會精緻;petals 不夠擴張,則不僅音量不夠、語調僵硬、音質也欠柔美。

QI＝EV＋EK＋FAAE

提昇實力，更上層樓：

對國內翻譯教育的期勉

在這個國際化的地球村中，各地區的政經文化互動頻繁，口譯員的需求快速增加。多所大專院校也開始設立口譯學程，口譯教育正蓬勃發展。然而我們目前的口譯教育仍面臨著若干挑戰與困境，其中最大的障礙就是師資不足以及口譯發展的方向不明確。

國際會議口譯員協會（AIIC）主席 Jennifer Mackintosh 女士，她曾表示我們最大的問題就是太多的空談理論，而不去加強師者本身的口譯實力。她更率直地指出口譯教學最重要的理論就是："You can't teach what you can't do!（自己不會口譯的人，怎能去教口譯呢！）" 歐洲委員會（SCIC）口譯總司 Brian Fox 先生則強調口譯教學者的三大必備條件是："Interpretation! Interpretation! And interpretation!（第一是要具備口譯能力，第二也是要具備口譯能力，第三還是要具備口譯能力！）" 他們的針砭真是一針見血，清楚地點出了我們口譯教學的兩大困境——師資不足和教學方向未明。

根據我個人以及許多國際具有豐富實戰經驗的口譯學者專家的工作與教學的經驗，口譯最基本的需要就是擁有極佳的 domain

language 以及 target language，在此之前，不宜進行口譯。因此，對於我們以中文為母語的人而言，口譯的訓練過程應該由會話口譯進為逐步口譯，再進為同步口譯。其中的竅門無他，**就是英語實力要快速提昇，以及學習口譯的方法需扎實有效**。無論教學同仁如何解釋，我們不得不承認一個事實：若是把我們個人的研究興趣或利益拿掉，口譯雖然是一項高深的技術，卻並非閉門造車的學問，**實踐才是最重要的**。儘管翻譯的種類眾多，但是，無論是溝通式的翻譯（communicative translation）、逐字翻譯（word for word translation）、語意翻譯（semantic translation）、意譯（free translation）、習慣用語式的翻譯（idiomatic translation）、直譯（literal translation…等等），儘管在 target language 和 source language 之間可以有上千上萬種研究題材，讓我們快樂地徜徉在自由而浩瀚的學術研究當中，但我再次呼籲，**對於學生而言，任何理論要避免光説不練，若不能提昇翻譯的實際操作，都僅是紙上談兵、隔靴搔癢，結果都將淪為空談**。

我曾數次和台灣和大陸的口筆譯教師共勉，我們首重自我提昇雙語以及翻譯的能力。其中的道理淺而易見："Like teacher, like pupil.（什麼樣的老師教出什麼樣的學生）"。教書是良心的工作，因為學生的職場如戰場，畢業生進入職場後，必將面對嚴厲的考驗，他們正如同走上戰場的士兵，需要的是優良堅固的武器、絕佳的策略和戰技，以及信心滿滿、昂首闊步的勇氣！所以翻譯教學必當使學子能實際動筆翻譯、開口傳譯，具有第一線口譯和筆譯的實力！

　　口譯必須具備快、準、美的基本特質、採擷雙語的精華、盡量使用純熟而道地的語言、符合譯文的文法與文化、迅速而輕鬆地傳遞給聽眾，並在必要時為原講者快速而不著痕跡地修飾或修補，為聽眾做最清楚而迷人的翻譯，甚至讓聽眾視「聽你的翻譯」為一場饗宴！

　　上乘的口譯必須將數個不同領域的知識和理論相融合在一起，淬煉成一個兼具廣度、深度及速度的技巧。卓越的翻譯人才，須具備下列能力：新聞英文寫作（因為新聞英文必須使用最精簡俐落的句型，而「速度」正是口譯所需）、語言學（必須使用到語言學的組織和表達技巧）、聲韻學（聲音的掌握對於是否呈現優美的口譯極具影響力）、舞台藝術（台風和個人魅力可為口譯大大地加分）、心理學（對於臨場、雙文化和正確的聽眾分析均能掌握）；當然還有最基本的──流暢俐落的雙語。

　　此外，如沐春風的口譯，除了展現文字之美、聲音之美之外，也須力求思緒清晰、反應迅速和完整流暢的表達，最後將能達到「心靈之美」的境界。期許我們一起努力，養成寬容的氣度、優美的氣質、穩健的台風、柔和善良之心、並謙遜有禮。在口譯界中，尤其不可急功近利、患得患失；同學之間彼此扶持、同業之間相知相惜，所謂「誠於中而形於外」，相隨心生，如此一來，口譯員將不只由「匠」成「才」，更可晉升為口譯的藝術家，進而在口譯的職場上展現大將之風、散發獨特的個人氣質，最後必能出類拔萃！

　　本書為個人多年口筆譯工作與教學的心得，我試著在教學與實際工作的經驗中研究出提昇翻譯教學的方法，希望兩岸的英語口筆譯教學更上一層樓。

　　敬祝各位教學同仁教學愉快，也祝福各位同學未來均以高分得到國際的翻譯證照。願神祝福你們。

2012 年 5 月於淡江大學

目次

實例 1　　In a Restaurant　在餐廳　　　1

　　實例 2　　In a Clinic　在診所　　　5

實例 3　　Making Dumplings　包水餃　　　9

　　實例 4　　Taking Care of Each Other　互相照顧　　13

實例 5　　Parents Went Out　自己看家　　17

　　實例 6　　Volcanic Eruptions　火山爆發　　21

實例 7　　Seeing a Fortune-Teller　算命　　25

　　實例 8　　Doing Mathematics　做數學　　29

實例 9　　Going to a Concert　聽音樂會　　33

實例 10　Math Applications (I)—Living Expenses
　　　　應用問題 (一)—計算生活費　37

實例 11　Math Applications (II)—Savings and Mortgages
　　　　應用問題 (二)—存款和貸款　41

實例 12　Self-Introduction 自我介紹　45

實例 13　The Cost of Living (Number Traning)
　　　　生活花費 (簡易數字訓練)　49

實例 14　Accurate Pronunciation 發音要標準　53

實例 15　Native Intonation 腔調要道地　57

實例 16　Posture 台風　59

實例 17　Delivering an Impromptu English Speech (I)
　　　　即席英語演講 (一)　63

實例 18　Delivering an Impromptu English
　　　　Speech (II) 即席英語演講 (二)　65

實例 19　Christianity 基督教　69

實例 20　Buddhism (I) 佛教 (一)　77

實例 21　Buddhism (II) 佛教（二）　81

　　實例 22　Losing Weight 減重　89

實例 23　A Joyful Heart Is the Best Medicine
　　喜樂的心乃是良藥　93

　　實例 24　Teeth Whitening 牙齒美白　97

實例 25　Why Has My Voice Turned Hoarse?
　　聲音為何變啞了？　101

　　實例 26　Eyestrain, Astigmatism and Myopia
　　　眼睛疲勞、散光和近視　111

實例 27　Immune from Depression
　　遠離憂鬱症　117

　　實例 28　Welcome to the Party! 你終於想通啦！　121

實例 29　Smoking Jeopardizes Health
　　抽菸有害健康　127

　　實例 30　Oral Hygiene 口腔衛生　133

實例 31　Very Annoying Tinnitus 惱人的耳鳴　139

實例 32　Cancer-Blocking 防癌　143

實例 33　I Loathe Cotics! 我對毒品深惡痛絕！　149

實例 34　Acquiring Immunity 增加免疫力　155

實例 35　The First Defence of Immune System
免疫系統的第一道防線　157

實例 36　Inflammation Makes the Body a War Zone
發炎使身體如戰場　161

實例 37　The Consequences of Inflammation
發炎的後遺症　165

實例 38　Zygote→Embryo→Fetus
受精卵→胚胎→胎兒　169

實例 39　Do Not Surrender to Your Fate!
扭轉命運！　175

實例 40　I.V. (Intravenous) 打點滴　177

實例 41　Cosmetic Surgeries (Plastic Surgeries)
整形　181

實例 42　Rhinoplasty (Nose Plastic Surgery) &
　　　　　Breast Augmentation 鼻子整形和隆乳　185

實例 43　Botox Injections 打肉毒桿菌　191

實例 44　Anesthesia 麻醉　195

實例 45　The Skills of Negotiating 談判技巧　199

實例 46　The Skills of Debating 辯論的技巧　205

實例 47　Don' Freak out, Moms and Dads!
　　　　　爸媽別抓狂！　211

實例 48　You Can Run the Show, Too!
　　　　　你也罩得住的！　217

實例 49　Rise above It! 看開點兒！　223

實例 50　Exuding Personal Magnetism
　　　　　散發個人魅力！　227

實例 51　Urban Space 都市土地　233

實例 52　Icebergs (I) 冰山（一）　239

實例 53　Icebergs (II) 冰山 (二)　　245

　　實例 54　Typhoons, Floods and Mudslides
　　　　　　颱風、洪水和土石流　　251

實例 55　The Greenhouse Effect on Earth (I)
　　　　　地球的溫室效應 (一)　　255

　　實例 56　The Greenhouse Effect on Earth (II)
　　　　　　地球的溫室效應 (二)　　259

實例 57　Air Pollution 空氣污染　　263

　　實例 58　The Ozone Layer 臭氧層　　267

實例 59　Teenagers, Parents and Schools
　　　　　孩子、父母和學校　　271

　　實例 60　US-China-Taiwan Relations
　　　　　　美-中-台關係　　275

實例 61　Taiwan (I)—Its History
　　　　　台灣 (一)——歷史　　279

實例 62　Taiwan (II)—Its Politics
台灣 (二) ——政治　285

實例 63　How Arabs See America (I) (The Cons)
阿拉伯人看美國 (一) (反對者的看法)　293

實例 64　How Arabs See America (II) (The Pros)
阿拉伯人看美國 (二) (支持者的看法)　299

實例 65　Al Jazeera 半島電視台　305

實例 66　US vs. NK (US Stance)
美國 vs. 北韓 (美國的立場)　309

實例 67　NK vs. US (NK's Stance)
北韓 vs. 美國 (北韓的立場)　313

實例 68　About Russia—A "Welfare" Policy
俄羅斯的「福利」法案　319

實例 69　Major Economic Policies on Mainland
China (I)　中國大陸的重要經濟政策 (一)　325

實例 70　Major Economic Policies on Mainland
China (II)　中國大陸的重要經濟政策 (二)　331

實例 71　An Appreciation of Renminbi Yuan
人民幣升值　335

實例 72　Zhejiang—One of the Richest Provinces
in China 浙江——富裕的一省　337

實例 73　Taiwanese Investments in China
台商投資中國大陸　341

實例 74　Singapore —A Quick Look
新加坡簡介　345

實例 75　The Depreciation of the American Dollar
美元貶值　351

實例 76　World Economy 世界經濟　355

實例 77　Japan —The Bubble Economy
日本—— 泡沫經濟　359

實例 78　Petroleum 石油　367

實例 79　Qingming Shang He Tu (Along the
River during the Ching-Ming Festival)
清明上河圖　371

實例 80　The Jadeite Cabbage 翠玉白菜　　375

實例 81　Patents 專利　　379

實例 82　Court Interpretation & Vocabulary
法庭口譯和重要字彙　　383

實例 83　A Model Court 模範法庭　　389

實例 84　Applying for a US Student Visa
申請赴美留學簽證　　393

實例 85　Obtaining a US Work Permit
美國工作許可　　397

附　錄　　401

訓 練 方 法

1. 可以看英文字彙，但絕對不要看書本最後的英文翻譯。

   ① 第一步：眼看中文、耳聽 CD，若第 2 遍仍不懂，可稍微翻一下英文，直到不看英文而聽懂為止。

   ② 第二步：眼看中文，開口和 CD 一起口譯，愈來愈快，直到和 CD 同步。

   ③ 口齒要清楚。

2. 本書的課程難易均等，所以讀者可依興趣或實際需要而自行選擇主題。

In a Restaurant

在餐廳

顧客：我們可以點菜了。

侍者：好的。你們要吃些什麼？

顧客：我要五分熟的牛排，配炸薯條，要脆一點的哦！
　　　對了，不要加味精。

侍者：沒問題。請問您要吃什麼甜點？我們有芒果布
　　　丁、香草冰淇淋，還有乳酪蛋糕。

（註：本書所採用的數字，並未經過考證，
　　僅供口譯訓練之練習。）

顧客：是免費的嗎？還是要另外付費？

侍者：甜點是隨餐附送的，飲料也一樣。

顧客：我有糖尿病，你們有沒有不加糖的點心？

侍者：我們有無糖的綠茶果凍，那是完全沒加糖的。

顧客：太好了。那我來一個無糖綠茶果凍和不加糖的玫瑰花果茶。

侍者：好！我們一下子就上菜了。

顧客：慢慢來，不急，我們打算在這裡至少耗一個半小時。

第一步　看中文聽英文；若有疑問，才參考書後的英文。（至少2次）

第二步　眼看中文，口中隨著 CD，練習中翻英。

第三步　不看中文、耳聽 CD，練習把英文翻成中文；若有疑問，才參考書中的中文。

1. 點菜 　　 order（若特別要和 buffet 區分，則可使用名詞：à la carte)。
例：Would you like buffet or à la carte?

2. 五分熟 　　 medium

3. 薯條 　　 French fries

4. 酥脆的 　　 crispy

5. 味精 　　 MSG

6. 甜點 　　 dessert

7. 芒果 　　 mango

8. 布丁 　　 pudding

9. 香草	vanilla
10. 免費奉送的	complimentary
11. 糖尿病	diabetes
12. 糖尿病人；糖尿病的	diabetic
13. 不加糖的	unsweetened 或 sugar free
14. 果凍	jello
15. 花茶	herbal tea
16. 慢慢來	take your time

In a Clinic

在診所

醫生：你哪裏不舒服？

病人：我嘔吐、兩手發抖、拉肚子、頭昏噁心，而且全身起紅疹！

醫生：你吃了些什麼不衛生的東西嗎？還是你對什麼食物過敏？

病人：昨晚去喝喜酒，我覺得那個配明蝦的蕃茄醬有一點發酸。

醫生：那麼其他的人有沒有和你類似的病狀？

病人：只有我是這樣。不過我平常就容易生病。

醫生：大概你的免疫力太低了。

病人：那怎麼辦？我都快昏倒了，我剛才來時，連路都走不穩！

醫生：現在我先給你打點滴。你回家以後要儘量每天運動，至少一週三次，一次至少半小時，而且要把汗流出來。這樣你不但讓你的內臟運動，也幫身體排毒。

第一步 看中文聽英文；若有疑問，才參考書後的英文。（至少 2 次）🎧

第二步 眼看中文，口中隨著 CD，練習中翻英。🎧

第三步 不看中文、耳聽 CD，練習把英文翻成中文；若有疑問，才參考書中的中文。🎧

1. 嘔吐　　　　　　　　throw up (*v.*)

2. 想吐　　　　　　　　feel like to throw up (*v.*)
　① feel like to　感到想⋯
　　例：I feel like to dance.
　　　　我感覺好想跳舞！
　② feel like + V-ing　感覺像⋯
　　例：I feel like dancing.
　　　　我感覺好像在跳舞。

3. 頭昏　　　　　　　　dizzy (*adj.*)

4. 腹瀉　　　　　　　　have a diarrhea

5. 感覺噁心、反胃　　　feel nauseated

6. 發抖　　　　　　　　shake

7. 紅疹　　　　　　　　rash

8. 衛生	hygiene
9. 衛生的	hygienic [ˋhaɪdʒɪˏɪn]
10. 過敏	allergic to (*adj.*)
11. 喜酒	wedding banquet
12. 明蝦	prawn
13. 蕃茄醬	ketchup
14. 免疫力	immunity
15. 昏倒	faint (*v.*)
16. 走路不穩	stagger
17. 點滴	I.V.
18. 出汗	sweat
19. 內臟	internal organ
20. 排毒	detoxify

Making Dumplings

包水餃

母親：我今天突然想吃鍋貼和水餃。要不要自己做些來吃？

女兒：好啊！我們先去超市買餃子皮，然後準備餡料。

母親：你想吃什麼餡？想吃韭菜豬肉餃子還是高麗菜牛肉水餃？還是又香又脆的鍋貼？

女兒：我們乾脆三種都做，好不好？

母親：那太麻煩了，而且我覺得鍋貼也太油膩了。我現在有高血壓，食物還是清淡一點兒好。

女兒：那我們來包瘦豬肉韭菜餃，裏面還要加冬粉、薑和蝦皮才香！

母親：好！今天的醬料就配大蒜、九層塔、蔥、麻油、醋、醬油。

女兒：還有辣椒醬，但是醬油用一點點就夠了，因爲裏面有防腐劑！

母親：再配個酸辣湯或玉米粥，怎樣？

女兒：媽！我口水都流出來了！

第一步 看中文聽英文；若有疑問，才參考書後的英文。（至少 2 次）🎧

第二步 眼看中文，口中隨著 CD，練習中翻英。🎧

第三步 不看中文、耳聽 CD，練習把英文翻成中文；若有疑問，才參考書中的中文。🎧

1. 鍋貼　　　　　pot sticker

2. 餃子皮　　　　dough

3. 餡　　　　　　filling

4. 韭菜　　　　　leeks

5. 高麗菜　　　　cabbage

6. 油膩　　　　　greasy

7. 高血壓　　　　hypertension

8. 冬粉　　　　　bean noodles

9. 薑　　　　　　ginger

10. 大蒜	garlic
11. 九層塔	basil
12. 麻油	sesame oil
13. 醋	vinegar
14. 醬油	soybean sauce
15. 防腐劑	preservative
16. 酸辣湯	hot and sour soup
17. 玉米粥	corn porridge

Taking Care of Each Other

互相照顧

夫： 我的喉嚨癢癢的。

妻： 冰箱有梨子，我再去買一點枇杷，聽説枇杷和梨子可以止咳化痰。

夫： 好啊，謝謝妳！妳眞是個好太太。

妻： 哪裏，過獎了。上次我便秘的時候，你還不是也幫我灌腸！

夫： 那是應該的。我們兩個年齡都大了，應該互相照顧。何況妳有偏頭痛的毛病，我的膽固醇也太高。我們不互相照顧的話，還能靠誰？

妻： 你講的真是一點都沒錯！我很感謝你一輩子對我忠誠。

夫： 哪裏，哪裏！我也很感謝妳和我同甘共苦一輩子。

第一步 看中文聽英文；若有疑問，才參考書後的英文。（至少 2 次）

第二步 眼看中文，口中隨著 CD，練習中翻英。

第三步 不看中文、耳聽 CD，練習把英文翻成中文；若有疑問，才參考書中的中文。

1. 癢　　　　itch (*v.*)

2. 梨　　　　pear

3. 冰箱　　　frig (= refrigerator)

4. 枇杷　　　loquat

5. 止咳　　　cease coughing

6. 化痰　　　dissolve phlegm

7. 便秘　　　constipation

8. 偏頭痛　　migraine

9. 膽固醇　　cholesterol

10. 雞皮疙瘩　goose bumps

Parents Went Out

自己看家

姊：今天爸媽都不在，我們把房子來個大搬風好不好？

妹：怎麼個搬法？

姊：妳把藤椅放到屏風旁邊，我把鋼琴推到搖椅和酒櫃中間。

妹：但是鋼琴好重，我們一起來搬好了。

姊：不用，下面有輪子啊！（*同學注意不能用 "wheels"）

妹：那我把廚房大掃除。我來洗水槽、碗櫥、砧板、電鍋和鍋蓋。

姊：好，那我把梳粧檯和馬桶、鏡子清乾淨。

妹：爸媽還真幸運有我們這種女兒！

姊：那妳上次和媽頂嘴，把她氣到快腦充血了，又怎麼說？

妹：妳還真是哪壺不開就提哪壺呢！

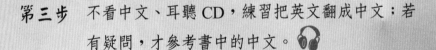

第一步　看中文聽英文；若有疑問，才參考書後的英文。（至少 2 次）

第二步　眼看中文，口中隨著 CD，練習中翻英。

第三步　不看中文、耳聽 CD，練習把英文翻成中文；若有疑問，才參考書中的中文。

1. 藤椅   rattan chair

2. 搖椅   rocking chair

3. 酒櫃   buffet

4. 屏風   screen

5. 小輪子   caster

6. 水槽   sink

7. 碗櫥   cupboard

8. 砧板   chopping board

9. 電鍋   rice cooker

10. 梳粧檯　　　　　　dresser

11. 腦充血　　　　　　apoplexy

6

Volcanic Eruptions

火山爆發

遊客：那座山怎麼在冒煙？

導遊：那是一座活火山，它自從 20 年前爆發過一次以後，就一直在冒煙。

遊客：我還以爲它是一座休火山呢。有沒有危險？如果爆發了，怎麼辦？

導遊：不用擔心。我們在這裏吃完午餐就要走了。

遊客：我上次看 *Discovery* 頻道，火山爆發時，岩漿都流到山下了，好可怕！

導遊：是啊。你知道很多研究火山的專家還走到火山口附近去觀察呢！

遊客：對呀。我上次看電視新聞，有兩位火山專家就是在火山爆發時被燒死了！

第一步 看中文聽英文；若有疑問，才參考書後的英文。（至少 2 次）🎧

第二步 眼看中文，口中隨著 CD，練習中翻英。🎧

第三步 不看中文、耳聽 CD，練習把英文翻成中文；若有疑問，才參考書中的中文。🎧

1. 火山	volcano
2. 死火山	extinct volcano
3. 休火山	dormant volcano (dormant: 休息的)
4. 活火山	active volcano
5. 岩漿	lava
6. 火山口	crater

7

Seeing a Fortune-Teller

算 命

命理師：你的眼睛又清又亮、鼻子又有肉，你一定又
　　　　聰明又有錢。

顧　客：可是我現在連房子都還沒有呢！我連買房子
　　　　的頭期款都沒有！

命理師：不急，不急。你的耳垂又大、人中又長，你
　　　　以後不但好命，而且還會長壽！

顧　客：真的？太好了！我會活到幾歲？什麼時候會發財？

命理師：我們算命的有一句話：「天機不可洩露」，時候到了你就知道了。不過你的牙齒太亂了，最好去整一整。

顧　客：可是矯正牙齒很貴耶，起碼要 2500 美元；而且我已經 25 歲了，還來得及整牙嗎？

命理師：當然來得及，這是永遠不嫌晚的。

顧　客：那你的命怎麼樣？怎麼不給自己算算？

命理師：早算過了，我就是個算命的命！

第一步　看中文聽英文；若有疑問，才參考書後的英文。（至少 2 次）🎧

第二步　眼看中文，口中隨著 CD，練習中翻英。🎧

第三步　不看中文、耳聽 CD，練習把英文翻成中文；若有疑問，才參考書中的中文。🎧

1. 有肉的　　　　　　fleshy (形容人)

2. 頭期款　　　　　　down payment

3. 耳垂　　　　　　　ear lobe

4. 人中　　　　　　　philtrum

5. 牙齒矯正器　　　　braces

6. 歪牙　　　　　　　snaggle teeth

7. 暴牙　　　　　　　protruding teeth

8. 獠牙　　　　　　　fang (例如吸血鬼之牙，或狗的牙，人類的犬齒則爲 canine tooth)

9. 門牙	front teeth
10. 臼齒	molar
11. 乳牙	milk teeth
12. 智齒	wisdom teeth

8

Doing Mathematics

做數學

A：天啊！又是數學課了！我真討厭數學！

B：為什麼？我覺得數學的世界真是有趣極了，尤其是解答了一個數學問題時，那種痛快真是筆墨難以形容！

A：我一想到三角形、正方形、長方形、菱形、梯形、面積、圓周就頭痛！

B：那是幾何！其實幾何也很有意思啊！看看從不同
　　形狀中算出它的面積或是體積……等等，也是蠻
　　具挑戰性的！

A：數字也很煩人！什麼偶數、奇數、平方、幾次方、
　　開根號……！（我們中文的習慣是「偶數、奇數」，英
　　文的習慣則是 "odds and evens"，次序相反！再者，中文習
　　慣說「爸爸媽媽」，英文則習慣說 "mom and dad"。）

B：其實你也不用煩心。你又不學理工，只要會用心
　　算或是用計算機做加、減、乘、除就行了。

A：最重要的是會做應用題，對不對？

B：答對了！對你來說，數學的意義正是如此！

第一步　看中文聽英文：若有疑問，才參考書後的英文。
　　　　　（至少 2 次）🎧

第二步　眼看中文，口中隨著 CD，練習中翻英。🎧

第三步　不看中文、耳聽 CD，練習把英文翻成中文；若
　　　　　有疑問，才參考書中的中文。🎧

可使用單字

1. 解答	solution	
2. 三角形	triangle	
3. 長方形	rectangle	
4. 菱形	rhombus	
5. 梯形	trapezium	
6. 面積	area	
7. 圓周	circumference	
8. 橢圓形	oval	
9. 圓心	origin	
10. 幾何	geometry	

(handwritten notes in right margin: 相鄰 oval; sector; cylinder; run; 球形 spheare)

11. 體積	mass
12. 偶數	even
13. 奇數	odd
14. 平方	square
15. 三次方	to the third power
16. 根號	square root
17. 計算機	calculator
18. 心算	mental arithmatics
19. 應用題	application

9

Going to a Concert

聽音樂會

A：嘿！我有兩張音樂會的票！今晚要不要一起去？

B：是誰的音樂會？該不會是世界三大男高音吧！

A：別作夢了！不過今晚的也不遜色哦！這是席琳狄翁的獨唱會！她有一個很棒的樂團來為她伴奏！那個指揮還是世界頂尖的指揮家呢！

B：真的？我簡直迫不及待了！

A： 電視上說她去年一年光是演唱會就賺了將近九億七千萬美元！

B： 天啊！我一個月才賺三百美元！真沒有天理！

A： 別這麼說！身體健康、知足常樂才是人間最可貴的生活呢！這樣想吧，你總不希望擔心被綁架吧！何況如果你那麼有名，連吃個臭豆腐都有人指指點點的，多難過啊！

B： 說的真對！何況我也沒他們的歌喉！

A： 這也是重點！我們還是今晚自由自在地先吃碗牛肉麵，再去聽她的演唱會吧！這樣的日子還真愜意呢！

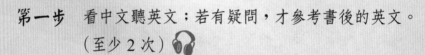

第一步　看中文聽英文：若有疑問，才參考書後的英文。（至少 2 次）

第二步　眼看中文，口中隨著 CD，練習中翻英。

第三步　不看中文、耳聽 CD，練習把英文翻成中文；若有疑問，才參考書中的中文。

可使用單字

1. 男高音   tenor

2. 退休   retire

3. 好遜！   It sucks!

4. 樂團   band

5. 伴奏   accompany

6. 指揮   conductor

7. 迫不及待   cannot wait

8. 綁架   kidnap

9. 贖金   ransom

10. 蚵   oyster

11. 臭豆腐　　　　　　　smelly tofu (或 pungent tofu)

12. 牛肉麵　　　　　　　beef noodles

13. 人生眞愜意！　　　　C'est la vie! (原是法文)
　　(或：哎！人生即是如此！)

---

* 基於愛護我們的飲食文化，筆者並不使用 stinky tofu 做為「臭
　　豆腐」之譯，正如同西方人所喜愛的「發霉的臭乳酪」，不會
　　使用 "moldy cheese"，而美其名為 "blue cheese".

Math Applications (I)
—Living Expenses

應用問題(一)
——計算生活費

A： 大衛每個月賺 900 美元，每個月要還車子貸款 200
美元、油錢 50 美元、房租 100 美元、健保費 20
美元、每天吃飯約 15 美元。哦！對了，還有每月
的娛樂費大約 30 美元，但他每年有一個半月的年

---

* 為了加強口譯的學習效果，部份數字依中文習慣，以國字寫出。

終獎金，你算算他每年可以存多少錢？

B：等一下，我去拿計算機……

1. 900 美元乘以 13.5 個月，等於一萬二千一百五十元，這是他全年的收入。我先把它記下來，等一下才不會忘。

2. 他每天吃飯 15 美元，乘以 365 天，等於 5,475 美元。

3. 他每個月車貸 200 美元、加上油錢 50 美元，再加房租 100 美元、健保費 20 美元、娛樂費 30 美元，一共是 400 美元，再乘以 12 個月，這就是他一年的花費，一共是 4,800 元。不對，還要加上伙食費 5,475 元，一共是一萬零二百七十五元。

4. 一年總收入 12,150 元扣掉一年的開銷 10,275 元，他每年可以存 1,875 元。

A：如果他想買房子呢？例如，房子是 20 萬美元，他買得起嗎？

B：我算算看。20 萬除以 1,875 元，等於 106.666……。哇！那太離譜了！要 106 年多才買得起？

A：可以貸款啊。我們來算一算利息！

B：算了，下次吧！我的頭已經發脹了！

第一步　看中文聽英文；若有疑問，才參考書後的英文。
　　　　（至少 2 次）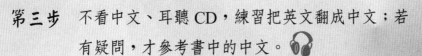

第二步　眼看中文，口中隨著 CD，練習中翻英。

第三步　不看中文、耳聽 CD，練習把英文翻成中文；若
　　　　有疑問，才參考書中的中文。

1. 數學的應用問題　　　application

2. 油錢　　　　　　　　gas

3. 健保費　　　　　　　health insurance
　　　　　　　　　　　(或是 medicaid insurance)

4. 計算機　　　　　　　calculator

5. 扣掉　　　　　　　　deduct

6. 娛樂費　　　　　　　entertainment fee

7. 房屋貸款　　　　　　mortgage

Math Applications (II)
—Savings and Mortgages

應用問題(二)
——存款和貸款

A：我們來做一個簡單的算數。

B：好啊！我去拿紙、筆和計算機。

A：假設房屋貸款 20 萬美元，每年利息 5%，利息要付多少？

B：我算算看！20 萬貸款×0.05 ＝ 1 萬元。

A：我是說一個月的利息。

B：哦，對了，還要除以 12 個月，等於 833.333 元。

A：答對了！我們再來做一個存錢的算數。如果你有 10 萬元放在銀行，年利率是 2%，一年以後連本帶利可拿回多少？

B：本金 10 萬乘以 1.02，等於 10 萬 2,000 元。

A：又答對了！

第一步 看中文聽英文；若有疑問，才參考書後的英文。（至少 2 次）

第二步 眼看中文，口中隨著 CD，練習中翻英。

第三步 不看中文、耳聽 CD，練習把英文翻成中文；若有疑問，才參考書中的中文。

1. 加上　　　　　　plus

2. 減掉　　　　　　minus

3. 乘以　　　　　　times

4. 除以　　　　　　divided by

5. 本金　　　　　　principal

6. 年利率　　　　　annual interest rate

　　　　　　　　　(或 yield rate)

實例

12

Self-Introduction

自我介紹

　　我來自鄉下。我的父親務農，我母親則是標準的家庭主婦，他們每天從早到晚都在為我們忙碌。

　　我姊姊現在二十三歲，去年大學剛畢業，到現在還沒找到工作，所以她的心情很鬱卒。我弟弟今年十七歲，還在念高二，他的功課很好，打算高中畢業後讀法律，因為他認為以後如果當律師不但錢賺得多，而且可以替無助的人伸張正義、又受人尊敬。但我並不完全贊同他的看法，我覺得他想的太天真了，因為聽說現在很多律師都賺不到錢，日子也過得很辛苦。

至於我自己，我所嚮往的一直就是文學和藝術。我從國中開始就喜歡畫畫和寫作，因此我現在念的是英文系。但是我覺得我的英文實在很菜，需要努力一番才行。

一個人要成功，需要努力、運氣和謹慎。我覺得我很幸運，因為我很努力，而且又碰到一位很棒的英文老師，她不但教導我學習優質英文的正確方向，使我的英文一天比一天好，而且她也教導我們要謹慎但快樂地走向人生之路，包括自律、注意健康和持有一顆喜樂、善良的心。

第一步 看中文聽英文：若有疑問，才參考書後的英文。（至少2次）🎧

第二步 眼看中文，口中隨著 CD，練習中翻英。🎧

第三步 不看中文、耳聽 CD，練習把英文翻成中文；若有疑問，才參考書中的中文。🎧

可使用單字

1. 鄉下	countryside
2. 鄉下土包子	bumpkin
3. 老土	geek
4. 宅男	home geek
5. 糊口	hand-to-mouth
6. 典型的	typical
7. 鬱卒	depressed
8. 正義	justice
9. 天真	naïve

10. 脫胎換骨	transform
11. 自律	self-discipline
12. 謹慎	prudent
13. 喜樂	cheerful

The Cost of Living (Number Traning)

生活花費 (簡易數字訓練)

　　曾幾何時，物價隨著通貨膨脹而調升，小到一枝鉛筆、大到一棟房子，都不知道貴了多少。例如，1980年代的大學學費一學期才幾百美元，現在卻要一、兩千元，再加上生活費、水電費、雜費、零用錢、房租……等開銷，一學期下來，我爸媽在我身上至少要花五千元。也就是説，我讀四年大學要花掉大約四萬元。我爸爸是公務員，我媽幾年前就被裁員，然後就一直失業在家，收入實在很有限。幸好我是獨生子（女），如果我還有兩、三個兄弟姊妹，後果真是不堪設想！

第一步　看中文聽英文；若有疑問，才參考書後的英文。（至少2次）

第二步　眼看中文，口中隨著 CD，練習中翻英。

第三步　不看中文、耳聽 CD，練習把英文翻成中文；若有疑問，才參考書中的中文。

可使用單字

1. 物價　　　　　　cost-of-living

2. 通貨膨脹　　　　inflation

3. 漲價　　　　　　hike

4. 水電費　　　　　utilities

5. 雜費　　　　　　miscellaneous

6. 零用錢　　　　　allowance

7. 房租　　　　　　rent

8. 公務員　　　　　official
　　　　　　　　　(或 government employee)

14

Accurate Pronunciation

發音要標準

　　在過去十年當中，全球的英語教學上有一個新的趨勢，就是非英語系國家人士在學習英語時，只有一個目標：能溝通就好；這個趨勢強調發音不用標準、腔調也不重要、甚至文法馬虎也無所謂。當然，也不需在意用字遣辭如何，即語言也無所謂是否優美！

　　的確，對任何人而言，要能精準地說出外國語言真的有些困難，更不用說要說得多流利了；但是我一直堅信，那些正值年輕、尚在求學階段、全身充滿活力、擁有活潑記憶力、且即將面對未來嚴格的職場考驗的同學們應該擁有最好的學習！尤其是英語系的學生更需要學習如何說寫極佳的英文，日後在職場上才能與人爭鋒，有機會脫穎而出；而他們日後如果成為英語教師，也才能真正為社會教育英才！

我曾經和一位熱愛中國文化的美國電台主管談到英語教學，他很客氣地認為中國學生學英文只求能說、聽懂即可，至於發音、腔調、文法皆毋需標準。他在英語教學上也並不嚴苛和挑剔，學生只要能有效地溝通就夠了，因為英語到底是他們的外國語文。我立刻問道：「那麼，你們電台會不會僱用一位英文能力很強，但是發音帶有中國腔的員工？」他毫不猶豫地說：「我們試過一次了，但是很多人寫信來表示不滿！」這番話不禁讓人感到惋惜，因為我們學生尚在求學階段，就被人放棄了。

第一步　看中文聽英文；若有疑問，才參考書後的英文。
　　　　（至少 2 次）

第二步　眼看中文，口中隨著 CD，練習中翻英。

第三步　不看中文、耳聽 CD，練習把英文翻成中文；若
　　　　有疑問，才參考書中的中文。

可使用單字

1.	趨勢	trend
2.	充滿活力的	dynamic
3.	職場	job market
4.	高階主管	high-ranking employee
5.	腔調	intonation
6.	具競爭力的	competitive
7.	毫不猶豫地	without a second thought

15

Native Intonation

腔調要道地

　　若要說出優美的英語，除了正確的發音，還要訓練腔調。我們學生早已習慣依照中文的一、二、三、四聲和輕聲來決定語調，但英文並沒有這樣的符號。所以，學生的英文句子是一律隨意而唸，結果語調不但呆板，而且雜亂刺耳！不正確的英語腔調的確是我們許多大專院校同學的通病。

　　學生努力學得一口優美的英語腔調之後，以後一定會發現這將多有助益。英文說得好，可美若行雲流水，否則學生說起英文就會像和尚唸經。基本上，語調是活的，它隨著說話者的心情而上下變動。幸好，同學在學習英文腔調時，基本上仍有若干軌跡可循，只要得其門而入，每一個學生都可以把英語說得收放自如，完全自在！

　　其實中國學生都應該學習正確的英語腔調，這是非常重要的。因爲對以英語爲母語的人士來說，他們都可藉由不同的腔調而知道，即使同樣一個句子，甚至短至同一個字，都可展現不同的生命和意涵。

第一步　看中文聽英文；若有疑問，才參考書後的英文。（至少 2 次）

第二步　眼看中文，口中隨著 CD，練習中翻英。

第三步　不看中文、耳聽 CD，練習把英文翻成中文；若有疑問，才參考書中的中文。

16

Posture

台　風

　　台風是現今每個專業口譯者都應該學習的。

　　我們有許多同學平時說起中文顯得活潑自信又機靈，一旦上台說英文，就完全變了一個人；活潑不再，取而代之的是僵硬；自信不再，取而代之的是自卑；機靈不再，取而代之的是呆滯。我個人認為這完全是一種心理障礙。不會說外文並非做錯事，是一件很正常的事，許多美國人不會說中國話，許多歐洲人不會

説英文，也不見他們因爲不擅説外文就表現得怯懦。

國人自清朝被西方的鴉片和大炮摧殘以來，我們就被國家和社會塑造出一種媚外崇洋的心理，誤導了許多學生學外語的心態：這種錯誤的觀念使我們學生好像只要在西方人的面前，不會説英文或是英文説得不夠好，就成了一件很尷尬的事，也正是這種心理障礙，使得我們的學生上台做英語演講或從事口譯時，成了苦事一椿，這是不正確的！無論話是説給誰聽，我們的言談內容、表情和感受都不要受到對方的國籍和社會地位的影響。

歸納起來，一個成功的口譯者站在台上時，應注意以下幾點風範與氣度：

1. 第一印象

2. 聲音控制

3. 儀態與姿勢

4. 裝扮

5. 同理心

6. 下台的風度

第一步　看中文聽英文；若有疑問，才參考書後的英文。
（至少 2 次）

第二步　眼看中文，口中隨著 CD，練習中翻英。

第三步　不看中文、耳聽 CD，練習把英文翻成中文；若
有疑問，才參考書中的中文。

Delivering an Impromptu English Speech (I)

即席英語演講(一)

　　許多演講比賽在決賽時，都會有即席演講，準備的時間通常約有 5～10 分鐘。我們來談談如何在三分鐘之內準備一篇上乘的講稿。

　　就即席演講而言，首要的仍是英文的實力。俗話說的好，「台上一分鐘，台下十年功」，對於中國學生來說，即席演講正是這樣的寫照。因此，在從事即席演講之前，同學要注意以下幾點：

1. 平時是否已累積相當廣泛的字彙？

2. 平時是否已有訓練說英文該有的極佳速度？

3. 平時是否已練就優雅從容的台風？

4. 發音是否標準？腔調是否道地？

5. 平時是否已學會極佳的發聲技巧，因此已具有清晰的咬字、迷人的音質、適當的音量，以及豐富的聲音表情？

第一步 看中文聽英文；若有疑問，才參考書後的英文。（至少2次）

第二步 眼看中文，口中隨著 CD，練習中翻英。

第三步 不看中文、耳聽 CD，練習把英文翻成中文；若有疑問，才參考書中的中文。

18

Delivering an Impromptu English Speech (II)
即席英語演講(二)

　　但是，並非具備了以上的雄厚實力，就一定能從事優質的即席演講，還必須注意以下幾個重點，才可以既快速又有效地上場：

　　首先，在拿到題目之後，迅速地依照以下的順序和時間做準備。

第一步→確定立場：先思考自己對演講講題將採取什麼立場或主題。心中的立場要清清楚楚，不能模糊，也不能說空話。（準備時間約 5-10 秒鐘）

第二步→原因：解釋自己爲何採取以上的立場和主題。（準備時間約 20 秒鐘）。

第三步→支持立場：根據你的記憶、你所認知的、你所觀察的、你所學的或是所想像的，找出活潑的例子來支持自己的想法（約 30 秒鐘），三分鐘的演講需要最少兩個、最多三個例子。

第四步→找單字：把《同步翻譯》帶在身邊，按照自己的需要迅速地找出 10～15 個生動的單字。不過同學平時即需熟背單字，在台上才可流利地說出（花 1 分鐘準備）。

第五步→找成語：從《同步翻譯》或是任何一本好的成語書中迅速地找出 2-3 個貼切的成語。再次提醒，這些成語平日就該讀熟了（花 20 秒鐘準備）。

第六步→快速作出大綱：（花 1～1.5 分鐘）用筆寫出
　　　　頭、中、尾三部份的關鍵字。

第一步　看中文聽英文；若有疑問，才參考書後的英文。
（至少 2 次）🎧

第二步　眼看中文，口中隨著 CD，練習中翻英。🎧

第三步　不看中文、耳聽 CD，練習把英文翻成中文；若
有疑問，才參考書中的中文。🎧

Christianity

基督教

A: 我認為所有的宗教都是一樣的,就是勸人為善!

B: 也不盡然。基督教追求真正自由自在的生命,但相信這種真正的自由自在並不是經由我們人類自己的努力而可得到。

A: 你所說的真正自由是什麼意思?

B: 人的愛、寬恕和憐憫之心都是有限的。而耶穌的愛和能力使我們舊人轉成新人，充滿了喜樂、愛、信心，因而終可獲得真正的自由心靈：不再憤怒、貪心，也不再說謊。

A: 基督教和天主教有何不同？

B: 這兩者很相似。但是就我所知，基督教比較不注重儀式，而且不是上教堂、做禮拜就夠了。

A: 那基督教到底是在做什麼？

B: 是讓基督主宰我們的生命。例如，人心只喜歡可愛之人，但耶穌卻原諒罪人，祂是神下凡，而且為了洗淨他們的罪而讓自己被釘十字架，成為祭祀品。

A: 不懂耶？

B: 正如同一般人不能用殘缺的牲畜或腐朽的蔬果來祭祀以討神歡心來替自己贖罪一樣，耶穌擺上祂自己完美無罪之生命，為全人類做一個大救贖。

A: 大多數的基督徒都很有愛心，不過有些是蠻差勁的。

B: 基督徒應該歡喜快樂地和他人分享神的無盡的愛和喜樂。那些做不到的人，其實是被耶穌斥為「偽君子」的！

第一步　看中文聽英文；若有疑問，才參考書後的英文。（至少 2 次）

第二步　眼看中文，口中隨著 CD，練習中翻英。

第三步　不看中文、耳聽 CD，練習把英文翻成中文；若有疑問，才參考書中的中文。

可使用單字

1. 基督教   Christianity

2. 打算   intend

3. 嶄新的   brand new

4. 儀式   ritual

5. 主要是   primarily

6. 上教堂做禮拜   churchgoing

7. 教條   creed

8. 行為   coduct

9. 有條件的   conditional

10. 十字架	cross
11. 罪人	sinner (基督教的名詞，一般社會上的罪犯是 criminal)
12. 罪	sin (不是殺人放火之 "crime"，而是各種有形無形之罪行罪念)
13. 殘廢的	handicapped
14. 腐朽的	decayed
15. 枯萎的	withered

有關宗教的其他重要單字：

16. 聖父	Holy Father

17. 聖子	Holy Son
18. 聖靈	Holy Spirit
19. 三位一體	trinity
20. 聖母瑪利亞	Virgin Mary
21. 門徒	disciple
22. 殉道者	martyr
23. 亞當	Adam
24. 夏娃	Eve
25. 守護天使	guardian angel
26. 萬能之神	Almighty God

27. 主日學	Sunday school
28. 恩典	grace
29. 讚美詩	hymn
30. 唱詩班	choir
31. 受洗	baptize
32. 彌撒	Mass
33. 禱告會	prayer meeting
34. 飯前禱告	say grace (*v.*)
35. 領聖餐	communion
36. 十字架	cross

37. 耶穌受難日	Good Friday
38. 復活	resurrect
39. 永生	etenal life
40. 十誡	the Ten Commandments
41. 魔鬼	Satan
42. 教皇	Pope
43. 紅衣主教	Cardinal
44. 摩門教	Mormonism
45. 摩門教徒	Morman

Buddhism (I)

佛教(一)

A: 在台灣這塊土地上，大多數的人是信佛的。到底佛教所信仰的是什麼？

B: 基本上來說，佛教所說的是人生之苦以及悲憫之心。

A: 他們拜眾神嗎？

B: 其實他們的教義是由佛祖釋迦牟尼所創的，佛教探索人間疾苦，而人之苦包括了生、老、病、死、挫敗，以及一切的歡樂都是短暫的。

A: 那麼，佛教有教導如何脫離這些苦難的方法嗎？

B: 也蠻難的，因為佛教相信人之所以為苦，乃在於與生俱來的貪、嗔、痴。

A: 我懂，例如對名利的渴望、對人或物的佔有之心，都導致我們生命中的恐懼、憤怒、忌妒、失望、甚至焦慮。

B: 真是不幸言中了，人生還真辛苦。

第一步　看中文聽英文；若有疑問，才參考書後的英文。（至少 2 次）🎧

第二步　眼看中文，口中隨著 CD，練習中翻英。🎧

第三步　不看中文、耳聽 CD，練習把英文翻成中文；若有疑問，才參考書中的中文。🎧

1. 佛教	Buddhism
2. 佛教徒	Buddhist
3. 探索	explore
4. 慈悲	mercy
5. 普遍的	universal
6. 短暫性	impermanence
7. 貪、瞋、痴	greed, hatred and delusion
8. 追求	craving
9. 感官享樂	sensual pleasure

10. 解脫	liberation
11. 涅槃	Nirvana [nɜˋvænə]
12. 了無牽掛	non-attachment

Buddhism (II)

佛教(二)

A: 依基督教和佛教來看，人之苦難如何才能止息？

B: 因爲基督徒的生命中有耶穌同行，所以不再焦慮，內心轉而充滿平靜；不再自私，心中轉而滿滿是愛；不再憤怒，變得願意寬恕人；而且不再恐懼，因爲生命中充滿了希望。

A: 而佛教徒則由修行而解脫？

B: 是的。佛教徒相信人要到「涅槃」時才能真正停止苦難，而他們的基本信念就是「輪迴」。

A: 我知道，輪迴就是「投胎轉世」之說，但什麼是「涅槃」？

B: 他們相信人必定經過許多生、老、病、死的轉世，直到某一世可以做到完全無慾無我之時，也就是「涅槃」（死亡）之時，才能終止生命之苦而得到真自由。

A: 所以「輪迴」就是「重生」？

B: 對，但是和因果有關。

A: 什麼因果？

B: 如果今世為善，下輩子就可能幸運地再投胎為人或者成為神明。

A: 如果種了惡果呢？

B: 如果今世為惡，下輩子則可能投胎轉世到低層次，例如變成豬或是變成一個餓鬼，甚至墜入地獄，永世不得超生。

A: 因此佛教徒會唸經、燒香、行善以為來世積陰德！

B:　我們必須承認，許多佛教徒是慈悲爲懷的，但也
　　有不少佛教徒所做的一切就是爲了下輩子有個好
　　光景。

第一步　看中文聽英文；若有疑問，才參考書後的英文。
　　　　（至少 2 次）

第二步　眼看中文，口中隨著 CD，練習中翻英。

第三步　不看中文、耳聽 CD，練習把英文翻成中文；若
　　　　有疑問，才參考書中的中文。

1. 投胎轉世   reincarnation

2. 狀態   state

3. 再生   rebirth

4. 因果   karma

5. 地獄   hell

6. 燒香   burn incense-sticks

7. 拜拜   worship god

8. 唸經   chant

9. 佛經   sutra

10. 陰德　　　　　　　　secret merit

有關佛教的其他重要單字：

11. 釋迦牟尼　　　　　Sakyamuni Buddha

12. 七情　　　　　　　seven emotions

13. 六慾　　　　　　　six carnal desires

14. 金剛經　　　　　　Diamond Sutra

15. 念珠　　　　　　　rosary

16. 齋戒　　　　　　　fast

17. 開齋　　　　　　　break fast (發音不是「早餐」)
　　　　　　　　　　　[brek] [fæst]

18. 開光	consecration
19. 達賴喇嘛	Dalai Lama
20. 達摩	Dharma
21. 觀世音	Goddess of Mercy
22. 城隍	City God
23. 肉身 (有別於靈魂時使用)	clod
24. 尼姑	nun
25. 托缽僧	mendicant (*n.*)
26. 化緣的	mendicant (*adj.*)
27. 苦修	mortify (*n.* mortification)

28. 大乘佛教   Mahayana
[mɑhə`jɑnə]

29. 小乘佛教   Hinayana
[hinə`jɑnə]

30. 前世   pre-existence, the previous
life

31. 今世   this life

32. 來世   afterlife

33. 尼姑庵   nunnery

34. 香客   pilgrim

35. 金箔紙、紙錢   foil

36. 布施之財物   alms

22

Losing Weight

減　重

A： 天啦，我真希望能夠在一禮拜之內就瘦個五公斤。

B： 健康的減重不見得就是最快的方法。

A： 我已經連續一個星期，天天跑步一小時了！

B： 我不贊成一個時髦的或一窩蜂的減胖計畫，也不
贊成一時興起節食、猛然增加運動量⋯⋯

A： 為什麼？醫生們不是都說要少吃多動嗎？

B：但是一切的改變需要漸進式的。

A：原來如此。

B：你知道運動本身就具防癌的效果嗎？

A：我知道。根據醫學報導，我們如果能持續性地多活動身體、飲食清淡，就可以比別人減少許多罹患癌症的機率。

B：那你對於催眠療法的看法如何？對減重有幫助嗎？

A：這方面我倒沒研究。

第一步 看中文聽英文；若有疑問，才參考書後的英文。（至少 2 次）

第二步 眼看中文，口中隨著 CD，練習中翻英。

第三步 不看中文、耳聽 CD，練習把英文翻成中文；若有疑問，才參考書中的中文。

可使用單字

1. 不見得	not necessarily
2. 慢跑	jog
3. 連續不斷	consecutive
4. 時髦的、一窩蜂的	trendy
5. 突發的	crash
6. 漸進的	gradual
7. 抗癌的	anti-cancer
8. 百分比	percentage
9. 催眠療法	hypnotherapy

A Joyful Heart Is the Best Medicine

喜樂的心乃是良藥

　　我曾看過一篇由台大醫院病理科知名的李豐醫師所寫的文章，提及她抗癌成功的心得。她每天早起之後，喝一大杯水清腸胃，再打坐 5 分鐘，然後吃五穀和水果的「排毒早餐」。

她不但每天運動，而且笑口常開。她説：「我們快樂時，細胞在顯微鏡底下看起來是又圓又亮。而我們情緒受到壓力時，細胞就會變得皺巴巴的。」

聖經有一句話説得很好：「喜樂的心，乃是良藥。憂傷的靈，使骨枯乾。」卡内基博士也曾説過，根據統計，我們所擔憂的事百分之九十九並不會發生。眞的，過個十年，回頭一望，當時所在意的一切都已過去了！智慧的人生實在就該是個喜樂的人生才對呀！

第一步 看中文聽英文；若有疑問，才參考書後的英文。（至少 2 次）🎧

第二步 眼看中文，口中隨著 CD，練習中翻英。🎧

第三步 不看中文、耳聽 CD，練習把英文翻成中文；若有疑問，才參考書中的中文。🎧

1. 病理科   pathology

2. 腸   intestine

3. 打坐   meditate

4. 五穀   grains

5. 細胞   cell

6. 皺   wrinkled, crumpled

7. 致癌的   carcinogenic

8. 致癌物   carcinogen

9. 防癌的   cancer-blocking

10. 使碎掉   crush

Teeth Whitening

牙齒美白

A： 我牙齒有點泛黃，想做漂白。

B： 潔白的牙齒看起來是比較怡人。你要到診所去做
　　 還是 DIY？

A： 診所是怎麼個做法？

B： 它是先把牙齒與口腔其他部位作隔離，再把一種
　　 強力的漂白劑放到牙齒上，然後再使用一種特別

的光線來幫助這個漂白劑發揮作用；這種方法對於牙齒上有色漬或是條紋的人較爲有效，通常不到一個小時就大功告成了。

A： 那 DIY 呢？

B： 就是製作一個適合口腔的小牙托，裏面裝滿了漂白劑，一天戴幾分鐘或幾個小時，然後幾天之內就可見到明顯的效果，而且比較經濟。

A： 效果可以維持多久？

B： 各種程度的效果會因人而異，但不幸的是，它的效果可能僅僅維持數個月而已，之後牙齒又會逐漸變黃。

第一步 看中文聽英文；若有疑問，才參考書後的英文。（至少 2 次）🎧

第二步 眼看中文，口中隨著 CD，練習中翻英。🎧

第三步 不看中文、耳聽 CD，練習把英文翻成中文；若有疑問，才參考書中的中文。🎧

可使用單字

1. 牙齒美白　　　　teeth whitening

2. 用得上　　　　　available

3. 漂白　　　　　　bleach

4. 漂白劑　　　　　bleaching agent

5. 隔離好的　　　　isolated

6. 色漬　　　　　　stain

7. 紋路　　　　　　streak

8. 強度　　　　　　intensity

9. 假牙　　　　　　　crown (套在真牙上的假牙，是
　　　　　　　　　　 false tooth 中最常見的一種)

10. 門牙　　　　　　　front teeth

Why Has My Voice Turned Hoarse?

聲音為何變啞了？

A： 我的聲音已經沙啞了一年多了。

B： 怎麼啦？

A：我去年初得了支氣管炎，卻還得繼續教書，加上四處演講。

B：所以你的聲帶沒得到休息！

A：到底聲音是如何變啞的呢？主要的原因是什麼？

B：通常不是聲帶就是控制聲帶的神經出了問題。

A：我覺得我的聲音有些微「粗嘎」和「漏風」。

B：呼吸困難嗎？

A：好得很。

B：你的脖子和耳朵附近有沒有硬塊？如果有硬塊，而硬塊已經存在了一段時間，摸起來硬硬的，就可能是癌；但是如果這個東西才長不久，摸起來是軟的，就可能是發炎了。

A：沒長硬塊。

B：抽菸和喝酒也可能造成聲音沙啞，但你既不抽菸又不喝酒！

A：對啊。

B：有沒有看醫生？

A： 看過兩位了，但是他們都囑咐我一定要禁聲十
　　天，這對我而言根本是不可能的事！

B： 那你就沒話說了！

第一步　看中文聽英文；若有疑問，才參考書後的英文。
　　　　　（至少 2 次）🎧

第二步　眼看中文，口中隨著 CD，練習中翻英。🎧

第三步　不看中文、耳聽 CD，練習把英文翻成中文；若
　　　　　有疑問，才參考書中的中文。🎧

可使用單字

1. 全面的   overall

2. 語調之高低   pitch (語調：intonation)

3. 相對地   relatively

4. 因素   factor

5. 觀察   perceive

6. 聲音粗糙   raspiness

7. 說話會漏風的   breathy (*n.* breathiness)
                                     [`brɛθɪ]

8. 形容詞   adjective

9. 吐氣	exhale
10. 吸氣	inhale

有關喉部的其他重要單字

1. 振動	vibrate
2. 本質上、基本上	essentially
3. 簧片	reed
4. 和……相似	analogous to [ə`næləgəs]
5. 改變	alter
6. 語言治療師	speech therapist (language therapist)

7. 喉頭	larynx
8. 聲帶	vocal cords
9. 肌肉的	muscular
10. 韌帶	ligament
11. 甲狀腺	thyroid [`θaɪrɔɪd]
12. 甲狀腺亢進	hyperthyroidism
13. 軟骨	cartilage [`kɑrtḷɪdʒ]
14. 喉節	Adam's apple
15. 座落於	situated

16. 氣管	trachea (= windpipe) [ˋtrekɪə]
17. 使人發嗆	choking
18. 可辨識的	recognizable

有關口鼻的其他重要單字

1. 口腔	oral cavity
2. 鼻腔	nasal cavity
3. 息肉	polyp [ˋpɑlɪp]
4. 扁桃腺	tonsils

5. 外傷	trauma
6. 整體配套中的一個活動	a coordinated activity
7. 上顎	palate [`pælɪt]
8. 口齒不清	slur
9. 一段期間當中	duration
10. 同樣地	similarly
11. 呼吸困難	have difficult breathing
12. 上網查詢	surf the web
13. 空氣通道	airway

14. 慢性的   chronic

15. 暴露於   exposure

16. 顯示   indication

17. 和⋯⋯有關   associated with

18. 不明原因的頭痛   unexplained headache

19. 發冷   chill

20. 夜晚盜汗   night sweats

26

Eyestrain, Astigmatism and Myopia

眼睛疲勞、散光和近視

A: 我眼睛好癢，而且感覺熱熱的，又長期有血絲，
裏面還有砂砂的感覺。

B: 你好像得了乾眼症候群。

A: 乾眼症？那怎麼辦？

B: 你的醫生可以開藥給你服用來減輕症狀。

A: 對了，我視力不太清楚，卻又沒有近視！

B: 那麼你可能有散光。

A: 散光到底是怎麼回事？

B: 你眼睛因折射不佳而使光線不能集中在眼睛裏的一個點上。

A: 所以東西看起來會歪七扭八的，而且視線也會變得模糊？

B: 沒錯。通常影像落在哪一點和你的散光到底是由近視或遠視所造成的有關。

A: 那麼眼睛要如何保養呢？

B: 不管看電視或用電腦時，每隔十五分鐘就要休息一下，才不會造成眼睛疲勞！

第一步　看中文聽英文；若有疑問，才參考書後的英文。
（至少 2 次）🎧

第二步　眼看中文，口中隨著 CD，練習中翻英。🎧

第三步　不看中文、耳聽 CD，練習把英文翻成中文；若
有疑問，才參考書中的中文。🎧

可使用單字

1. 癢   itch

2. 感覺有砂   gritty (*adj.*)

3. 有砂砂的感覺   grittiness (*n.*) (一般情況均可使用，例如眼睛砂砂的、食物有砂)

4. 乾眼症   dry eye

5. 症候群   syndrome

6. 眼科醫生   ophthalmologist [ˌɑfθæl`malədʒɪst]

7. 開處方   prescribe

8. 減輕 (痛苦)	alleviate [ə`livɪet]
9. 視力	vision
10. 眼花了	vision is blurred
11. 有近視的	near-sighted (*adj.*)
12. 近視	myopia (*n.*)
13. 散光	astigmatism
14. 折射	refractive [rɪ`fræktɪv]
15. 折射率	refrative index
16. 歪曲變形	distortion (*adj.* distorted)
17. 和……有關	be associated with

18. 遠視	hyperopia
19. 眼睛疲勞	eyestrain
20. 老花眼	presbyopia
21. 老花眼鏡	reading glasses

27

Immune from Depression

遠離憂鬱症

A: 爲什麼我們周圍有愈來愈多的人患憂鬱症？

B: 因爲經濟不景氣、失業率增高、人際關係不協調、
人心脆弱，使現今社會愈來愈多的人內心時感焦慮。

A: 我們該如何自救呢？

B: 人生苦短，不要爲過去的事情後悔，也不要爲未
來的事情恐慌。學習感恩，並活在當下。

A: 可是我一有壓力就開始鑽牛角尖。

B: 那你就多運動。運動可以讓我們身體分泌一種奇妙的「腦內啡」，讓我們感覺舒服，並可預防或對抗憂鬱症。

A: 但是我的目標還沒達到，我放鬆不了！

B: 不要把目標定得太高；每達到一個小目標就可以好好慶祝一番。

A: 我喜歡獨處。人是不是一定要有社交呢？

B: 努力讓自己去看看喜劇電影，或和朋友去餐廳吃餐飯，說出你的感受，然後儘量開懷大笑！

第一步 看中文聽英文；若有疑問，才參考書後的英文。（至少 2 次）🎧

第二步 眼看中文，口中隨著 CD，練習中翻英。🎧

第三步 不看中文、耳聽 CD，練習把英文翻成中文；若有疑問，才參考書中的中文。🎧

1. 憂鬱症　　　　　　　depression (= melancholia)

2. 躁鬱症　　　　　　　anxiety disorder

3. 減壓　　　　　　　　reduce stress

4. 社交　　　　　　　　socialize

5. 心靈團體　　　　　　support group (一群人坐在一起談起自己壓力來源的一個專業團體)

6. 失業率　　　　　　　unemployment rate

7. 鑽牛角尖　　　　　　split the hairs

8. 當下　　　　　　　　état-d´être (英直譯爲 state of being) [`eda`dɛtr] (註：r 唸「喝」的音)

28

Welcome to the Party!

你終於想通啦！

A： 我兒子下個月要結婚了，我的內心眞是百感交集。我是不是要失去他了？

B： 「失去」並不是個很恰當的字眼。他並不是你的資產，而且他得要自己去闖盪人生。

A： 但他是我的骨肉啊！

B： 聖經上說：「人要離開父母，與妻子結爲一體。」你也不能再干涉他生活上的點點滴滴了。

A： 我聽了好難過。難道我連他們和哪些朋友在一起、收入多少，都不能過問嗎？

B： 還不只如此。如果他們沒常來看你，你也不要埋怨；另外，如果他們家人有什麼活動，你也不要期盼跟著去；若要帶你去，他們自然會開口。

A： 如果我的媳婦做錯事了，怎麼辦？

B： 那也不關你的事。可能是你的兒子做錯了呢？你要做個和平的使者，不可挑撥離間，千萬不要讓自己成為他們背上的芒刺！

A： 但是每天看不到他，我會覺得悵然若失！

B： 孝順是件美事，而且會深受祝福，但它是勉強不來的。你不妨自己交些朋友，培養一些嗜好，你會發現和朋友在一起比和孩子在一起更有意義！

A： 那我要不要三不五時去討好我的媳婦呢？

B： 那可真是一件吃力不討好的事！不過如果你該稱讚她的時候，就要大方地稱讚她；該感謝她時，就要表示謝意。

A： 所以，我就得過自己的日子，然後明哲保身？這
多痛苦啊！

B： 你終於想通啦！但也不妨這麼想：說不定你會有
全天下最好的兒子和媳婦呢！

第一步　看中文聽英文；若有疑問，才參考書後的英文。
（至少 2 次）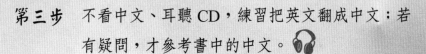

第二步　眼看中文，口中隨著 CD，練習中翻英。

第三步　不看中文、耳聽 CD，練習把英文翻成中文；若
有疑問，才參考書中的中文。

1. 內心五味雜陳	be tangled with a multitude of feelings
2. 自己闖天下	blaze one's own trail
3. 有資格去……	be entitled to …
4. 不常	infrequent
5. 行為不當	misbehave
6. 和事佬	peacemaker
7. 挑撥離間	sow discords
8. 眼中釘	eyesore

9. 孝順	filial piety
10. 自願的	voluntary
11. 有回報的	rewarding
12. 討好	please (*v.*)
13. 吃力不討好的	taxing and thankless
14. 稱讚	compliment (*v.* & *n.*)
15. 該有的	due
16. 少管閒事、少惹事	keep one's nose clean
17. 可憐的	miserable
18. 事情往好處想	think on the bright side

Smoking Jeopardizes Health

抽菸有害健康

A: 我有一個朋友 42 歲時就因肺癌而過世了。他在世時經常抽菸，而且悲哀的是，他工作時又經常暴露在二手菸的環境裏。

B: 的確如此！研究發現，在美國，女性也要注意防範肺癌。目前已知的是，死於肺癌的女性中有百分之九十都抽菸。

A: 我也聽說美國死於肺癌的女性多過死於乳癌。

B: 癌到底是什麼？我只知道那是惡性腫瘤。

A: 癌症是當我們某些細胞無法正常運作，而且增生很快、產生太多的組織時，最後所形成的腫瘤。

B: 我們都知道要預防肺癌的最佳方法就是戒菸。

A: 是的。我們愈早戒菸，對自己及別人都會好。你知道如果在手術後抽菸會影響傷口的癒合嗎？

B: 那倒還未曾聽說！

A: 因為香菸會使我們的血管收緊，導致血液的流量減少。如果手術是全身麻醉的話，在手術後癒合期抽菸可能會讓你咳嗽，造成內出血！

第一步　看中文聽英文；若有疑問，才參考書後的英文。（至少 2 次）

第二步　眼看中文，口中隨著 CD，練習中翻英。

第三步　不看中文、耳聽 CD，練習把英文翻成中文；若有疑問，才參考書中的中文。

1. 干預　　　　　interfere with

2. 收緊　　　　　constrict

3. 血管　　　　　blood vessel

4. 減少　　　　　decrease

5. 血流　　　　　blood flow

6. 一氧化碳　　　carbon monoxide

7. 傷口　　　　　wound

8. 內出血　　　　internal bleeding

9. 肺癌　　　　　lung cancer

10. 圓錐體	cone
11. 器官	organ
12. 呼吸系統	respiratory system
13. 二手菸	second-hand smoke
14. 腫瘤	tumor
15. 組織	tissue
16. 顯微鏡	microscope
17. 蔓延	spread
18. 乳癌	breast cancer
19. 關心	concerned about

20. 二氧化碳　　　　　carbon dioxide

Oral Hygiene
口腔衛生

A: 我的臼齒好痛，可能是蛀牙了！

B: 你上次什麼時候看牙的？

A: 兩年前。

B: 你應該每半年去洗一次牙。我們人就像一部機器，年紀愈大毛病就愈多。因此，當我們年齡愈大時，就愈會發現各種老化的現象。

A: 你說得一點都沒錯!我已經發現歲月催人老了:
包括白髮增加、皺紋出來了、黑斑也出現了,還
有從前都好好的,現在卻常常這裏痛、那裏痛……
等等。

B: 同樣的,我們的口腔也會受到老化的影響。你知
道細菌在我們的牙齒、牙齦、嘴唇、舌頭上甚至
喉嚨裏不斷地活動嗎?

A: 那我該怎麼把這些細菌殺死呢?

B: 有些細菌是無害的,甚至有一些還對我們身體有
益。只有某些種類的細菌會依附在我們牙齒表面
的琺瑯質上,如果這些細菌沒有被清除的話,就
會在短時間內成倍數成長。

A: 然後就形成牙垢?

B: 差不多。因爲甚至連我們口中的唾液中所含的蛋
白質也會加入,形成一層帶有白色的薄膜,覆蓋
在牙齒上。這一層膜就是牙垢,會引起蛀牙。

第一步　看中文聽英文；若有疑問，才參考書後的英文。
（至少 2 次）

第二步　眼看中文，口中隨著 CD，練習中翻英。

第三步　不看中文、耳聽 CD，練習把英文翻成中文；若
有疑問，才參考書中的中文。

1. 口腔衛生　　　　　　　oral hygiene

2. 老化　　　　　　　　　aging

3. 皺紋　　　　　　　　　wrinkles

4. 白髮　　　　　　　　　grey hair

5. 年齡漸長　　　　　　　advancing age

6. 進行　　　　　　　　　undergo

7. 微妙的　　　　　　　　subtle

8. 明顯而被醫生宣判的　　pronounced (*adj.*)
   (疾病)

9. 細菌	bacteria
10. 群體	colony
11. 微生物	living organisms
12. 牙齦	gum
13. 琺瑯質	enamel [ɪˋnæml̩]
14. 以倍數成長	multiply and grow in number
15. 唾液	saliva
16. 薄膜	film
17. 蛀牙	cavity

Very Annoying Tinnitus

惱人的耳鳴

A: 我耳鳴，好難受哦！

B: 你有沒有看耳鼻喉科？

A: 有啊，醫生説我缺少維他命 B12。爲什麽耳鳴會和 B12 有關？

B: 因爲耳鳴和神經有關，而只要談到神經，就不能不談到維他命 B12。

A: 不懂。

B: 當我們缺少維他命 B12 時，我們血液中就會增加一種對神經有毒的氨基酸。

A: 有多少的人因為缺乏維他命 B12 而飽受耳鳴之苦？

B: 確切的數字我不是很清楚，但大約有百分之十到二十的耳鳴患者都缺乏維他命 B12。你知道嗎？長期暴露在噪音當中可能也會損耗我們體內的維他命 B12！

A: 那不就形成了惡性循環？

B: 對。攝取足量的維他命 B12，少拿棉花棒挖耳朵、不要經常使用隨身聽、而且音樂關小聲點。

第一步　看中文聽英文；若有疑問，才參考書後的英文。（至少 2 次）🎧

第二步　眼看中文，口中隨著 CD，練習中翻英。🎧

第三步　不看中文、耳聽 CD，練習把英文翻成中文；若有疑問，才參考書中的中文。🎧

可使用單字

1. 耳鳴   tinnitis

2. 養分   nutrient

3. 使絕緣   insulate
[`ɪnsəlet]

4. 導 (電)   conduct

5. 缺少的   deficient

6. 有毒的   toxic

7. 反射   reflexes

8. 不良的   impaired

9. 察覺	perception
10. 誘導	induce
11. 毫克	microgram
12. 注射	injection
13. 暴露	exposure
14. 耗盡	deplete [dɪ`plit]
15. 脆弱的、易受傷害的	vulnerable
16. 隨身聽	walkman

Cancer-Blocking

防　癌

A: 怎麼愈來愈多的人罹患癌症？到底是怎麼回事？

B: 其實，大多數的癌症是可預防的，只要我們在每天的生活中做一些適度的改變即可。

A: 我知道。早在 30 年前，美國一個機構就有一份重要的研究報告指出，近百分之七十的癌症是和我們的生活習慣有直接的關係。而現在這個數字比以前更高了！

B: 空氣污染、水污染、農藥、抗生素、用在動物身上的生長激素……等，都在對我們的身體下毒！

A: 那我們就更需要運動不可了，因爲癌細胞在充分的氧氣中是無法生存的。

B: 吃的健康可以幫助我們遠離各種癌症。你知不知道有哪些蔬菜水果可以防癌？

A: 我知道的有十字花科蔬菜類的東西，包括綠花椰菜、花菜、白蘿蔔……等。

B: 還有各種深色蔬菜、乾燥的堅果食物、地瓜、薑、大蒜、仙人掌科植物、藍莓、奇異果、火龍果、洋蔥和蕃茄。

第一步　看中文聽英文；若有疑問，才參考書後的英文。（至少 2 次）🎧

第二步　眼看中文，口中隨著 CD，練習中翻英。🎧

第三步　不看中文、耳聽 CD，練習把英文翻成中文；若有疑問，才參考書中的中文。🎧

可使用單字

1. 適度的   moderate

2. 機構   institute

3. 調整   adjustment

4. 心臟病   heart disease

5. 中風   stroke

6. 高血壓   hypertension

7. 糖尿病   diabetes

8. 生長激素   growth hormone

9. 香菸、菸草   tobacco

10. 任何型態的	in any form
11. 誇大的	whopping
12. 和……有關	linked to
13. 胰臟	kidney
14. 膀胱	bladder
15. 頸部	cervix
16. 前列腺	prostste
17. 結腸	colon
18. 直腸	rectum
19. 有……能力	potentially

20. 十字花科蔬菜	cruciferous vegetable
	(= crucifer)
21. 綠花椰菜	broccoli
22. 花菜	cauliflouer
23. 甘藍菜	kale
24. 小豆（綠豆、紅豆、黃豆類）	beans
25. 豌豆	peas
26. 大蒜	garlic
27. 薑	ginger
28. 柑橘類	citrus

29. 藍莓	blueberry
30. 柚子	pomelo [`paməlo]

I Loathe Cotics!

我對毒品深惡痛絕！

A: 你要不要嘗試一下搖頭丸？

B: 打死我也不幹！

A: 我想嚐嚐看能否提神。聽説搖頭丸可以促進我們
肌肉的協調性，而且讓我們歡愉！你只要想想它
在坊間的別名：「忘我」和「擁抱」，就知道它有
多迷人了。

B: 我知道的還不只這些，它還被叫做「愛的活力」以及「XTC」。

A: 眞的假的？我還以爲你是老土呢！

B: 我不是老土，只是沒笨到把自己變成一個倒霉鬼而已。

A: 拜託！沒那麼嚴重啦！搖頭丸一吃下肚，壓力就消失了，還會感到飄飄然喔！何況，吃一點點又不會上癮。

B: 有毒癮的人剛開始都是這麼遊説別人的，他們不擇手段拖人下水；你要被洗腦，悉聽尊便，我是不會上當的。

A: 但是吃了搖頭丸會内心平靜哦！

B: 研究證明，搖頭丸會讓人神經中毒，而且因爲主要的傷害在腦部，所以也會影響情緒、進取心、睡眠。我可不想十幾歲就開始減低記憶力。

A: 它也會危害生理嗎？

B: 當然！它會造成肝、腎以及心血管衰竭。

A: 太恐怖了！但是當我沮喪、緊張或是感到焦慮時，該怎麼辦呢？

B: 你得學些壓力處理的技巧，且絕對不要鑽牛角
尖！

A: 而且還要少吃多動，才能排毒？

B: 沒錯！

第一步　看中文聽英文；若有疑問，才參考書後的英文。
（至少 2 次）🎧

第二步　眼看中文，口中隨著 CD，練習中翻英。🎧

第三步　不看中文、耳聽 CD，練習把英文翻成中文；若
有疑問，才參考書中的中文。🎧

可使用單字

1. 痛恨　　　loathe

2. 搖頭丸　　ecstasy (或 MDMA)
　　　　　　[ˋɛkstəsɪ]

3. 意亂情迷　ecstasy

4. 安非他命　amphetamine
　　　　　　[æmˋfɛtəmin]

5. 精神一振　kick

6. 老土　　　geek
　　　　　　[gik]

7. 土土的　　geeky

8. 可憐人	unfortunate (*n.*)
9. 不擇手段	by hook or by crook
10. 使人上癮，使人上鉤	hook…up
11. 把人拖下水	drag…in
12. 洗腦	brainwash (*v.*)
13. 肝	liver
14. 腎	kidney
15. 心血管方面的	cardiovascular (*adj.*) [kardɪoˋvæskjələ˞]
16. 衰竭	failure
17. 鑽牛角尖	split hairs

34

Acquiring Immunity

增加免疫力

　　我最近看了兩本書，一本是林光常醫師寫的《無毒一身輕》，另一本是一位希臘藍寧士醫師所寫的《來自身體的聲音》。我覺得這兩本書非常好，因為它們提醒我們如何照顧自己的身體。其中我認為最重要的是我們對於免疫系統應該有的認識。

　　首先，並不是所有的感冒都要吃藥、打針。我們的身體只要有本錢，就具有非常神奇的自療的能力，重要的是我們要如何讓我們的本錢——免疫系統發揮最大的作用！

這兩本書都提到一個現行普遍的養生觀念，也就是，我們的生命中有三樣東西決定了我們是否健康：飲食、身體、心靈，因為這三樣東西決定了我們的免疫系統到底可以變得有多強或者有多弱。

第一步　看中文聽英文；若有疑問，才參考書後的英文。（至少 2 次）🎧

第二步　眼看中文，口中隨著 CD，練習中翻英。🎧

第三步　不看中文、耳聽 CD，練習把英文翻成中文；若有疑問，才參考書中的中文。🎧

The First Defence of Immune System

免疫系統的第一道防線

　　根據藍寧士醫師所說，我們免疫系統的第一層是皮膚。這個皮膚不但包括了身上的皮膚，還包括鼻、口及消化道內部的組織黏膜，例如鼻涕和唾液。皮膚的功能之一是保護我們不受外界的侵襲，但我們卻經常傷害它。例如，我們喝水不夠而使喉嚨乾燥，就沒有足夠的黏液和唾液來阻擋病毒入侵；吃得太冷、太熱、太辣，或說話太多、大喊大叫、喝酒、吃味精……都會傷害我們的喉嚨；或是在冷氣房太久而使口、鼻乾燥……，在在都減弱我們免疫系統的第一道防線。

所以，一定要多喝水，好好照顧我們的皮膚，包括口、鼻……等，我們第一道的免疫防線就建立起來了。

第一步　看中文聽英文；若有疑問，才參考書後的英文。（至少 2 次）

第二步　眼看中文，口中隨著 CD，練習中翻英。

第三步　不看中文、耳聽 CD，練習把英文翻成中文；若有疑問，才參考書中的中文。

可使用單字

1. 消化系統   digestive system

2. 消化器官   digestive organ

3. 鼻涕   mucus

4. 口水   saliva

5. 病毒   virus

6. 味精   MSG

7. 防線   defence

8. 減弱   weaken

實例

36

Inflammation Makes the Body a War Zone

發炎使身體如戰場

　　大概很多人都不會想到，要保持健康身體的第二道防線就是不要發炎！

　　藍醫師在他的書中提到，發炎就是體內的戰爭，使身體如戰場：飽受戰爭的破壞。我們的身體某一部份發炎時，免疫系統就會來對抗它。不幸的是，同時也會破壞我們健康的細胞，例如紅斑性狼瘡症、牛皮癬、甲狀腺疾病……等等，對了，還包括癌症，都屬於發炎。

藍醫師說，若不好好處理這種發炎現象，就會拱手讓許多疾病得勝！

第一步 看中文聽英文：若有疑問，才參考書後的英文。（至少 2 次）🎧

第二步 眼看中文，口中隨著 CD，練習中翻英。🎧

第三步 不看中文、耳聽 CD，練習把英文翻成中文；若有疑問，才參考書中的中文。🎧

1. 發炎   inflammation

2. 發炎了   inflamed

3. 關節炎、痛風   arthritis

4. 紅斑性狼瘡症   lupus (全名是 erythematosus

                                    [ˋlupəs]   [ɛrıˋthiməˋtɑsəs])

5. 牛皮癬、乾癬   psoriasis

                                    [səˋraıəsıs]

6. 傳染病   epidemic

7. 甲狀腺   thyroid

8. 有毒的	toxic
9. 貧血	anemia
10. 風濕	rheumatism [`rumətɪzm]
11. 萎縮	atrophy (例如肌肉、神經的萎縮)

The Consequeuces of Inflammation

發炎的後遺症

　　另外，藍醫師和林醫師還提到我們所吃、所用的東西都會造成身體不同程度的發炎，這些東西包括防腐劑、殺蟲劑、人工色素、人工香料、自由基、被污染的空氣和水，以及各種蛋、肉、海鮮……等過敏性食物。所以，我們一定要小心飲食，儘量減低飲食中所含的毒素。

書中都提到，身體發炎的初期會造成各種症狀，例如疲倦、頭昏、鼻塞、皮膚起紅疹、發癢、咳嗽、皮膚炎、長濕疹、甚至心理和精神方面的不適：疾病還有沮喪、肥胖、高膽固醇、血糖不穩、糖尿病、荷爾蒙不平均、心血管疾病、中風、背痛、關節炎……等。

這兩位醫師警告，到了免疫系統全面受損時，不只這些過去所曾出現的情況會更糟，還會出現新的疾病，例如胃潰瘍、癌症、婦科疾病、牙齒毛病、老年痴呆及其他的老化現象……。

天啊！這麼多疾病！我們為了保護第一道和第二道防線，真的要多喝水、多休息、注意飲食、少出入細菌多的場所，還有最重要的就是時常歡喜快樂。

第一步　看中文聽英文；若有疑問，才參考書後的英文。（至少 2 次）🎧

第二步　眼看中文，口中隨著 CD，練習中翻英。🎧

第三步　不看中文、耳聽 CD，練習把英文翻成中文；若有疑問，才參考書中的中文。🎧

1. 後遺症   sequela (大多用複數：sequelae)

                 [sɪˋkwilə]   [sɪˋkwili]

2. 防腐劑   preservative

3. 殺蟲劑   insecticide

4. 人工色素   artificial pigment

5. 自由基   free radicals

6. 疲倦   fatigue (*n.*)

                 [fəˋtig]

7. 鼻塞   stuffy nose

8. 皮膚炎　　　　　　　　dermatitis (——itis [`aɪtɪs]表示
　　　　　　　　　　　　[ˌdɜməˋtaɪtɪs]　　　　　　發炎)

9. 濕疹　　　　　　　　　eczema
　　　　　　　　　　　　[ˋɛksɪmə] 或 [ɪgˋzimə] 都常用

10. 沮喪　　　　　　　　　depression

11. 肥胖（病）　　　　　　obesity

12. 分泌　　　　　　　　　secretion

13. 關節炎　　　　　　　　arthritis

14. 胃潰瘍　　　　　　　　gastric ulcer

15. 老年痴呆　　　　　　　Alzheimer's disease
　　　　　　　　　　　　[alˋzaɪmə]

Zygote→Embryo→Fetus

受精卵→胚胎→胎兒

　　男性的睪丸會製造精子，女性的卵巢則在女性出生時就已擁有 3 到 4 萬個卵子，這也解釋了為什麼高齡產婦必須小心的原因了。因為卵子自始就一直貯存於卵巢內，而經由歲月中所遭遇的輻射物（例如 X 光照射、空氣和化學污染、受傷、老化……等因素就愈來愈不健康了。

卵子和精子結合後，成爲受精卵，裏面就含有DNA，而我們人類所有的特徵都受 DNA 所控制，也就是我們所説的「基因」。DNA 裏面的染色體不但決定了我們的性別，也在卵子和精子結合爲受精卵的那一刻，就決定了我們的膚色、高矮、面容、頭髮的顏色、直髮或鬈髮、甚至個性和疾病。

醫學界已證實，受遺傳所影響的疾病包括糖尿病、血友病、精神病、蒙古痴呆症、過敏，甚至癌症以及許多心血管疾病。幸好，羊水穿刺術（婦女最後一次月經之後的 15～18 週）和絨毛膜取樣術（10～12 週）可以提前知道是否有染色體和遺傳的先天缺陷；我們東方人則喜歡用這兩種科技來做胎兒的性別測試。

第一步 看中文聽英文；若有疑問，才參考書後的英文。（至少 2 次）🎧

第二步 眼看中文，口中隨著 CD，練習中翻英。🎧

第三步 不看中文、耳聽 CD，練習把英文翻成中文；若有疑問，才參考書中的中文。🎧

1. 胎兒   fetus

2. 睪丸   testicles (= testes)

3. 精子   sperm

4. 卵巢   ovary

5. 卵子   ovum

6. 魚卵   spawn

7. 老化   aging

8. 受精   fertilize

9. 受精卵	zygote [ˋzaɪgot]
10. 胚胎	embryo
11. 基因	gene
12. 染色體	chromosome [ˋkromə͵som]
13. 性別	gender
14. 血友病	hemophilia (hemo—血 [himəˋfɪlɪə]　philia—愛)
15. 精神疾病	mental diseases
16. 蒙古症	Mongolian idiocy
17. 心血管疾病	cardiovascular disease

18. 羊水穿刺術   amniocentesis
[͵æmnɪosɛn`tisəs]

19. 絨毛膜取樣術   CVS (Chorionic villus sampling)

Do Not Surrender to Your Fate!

扭轉命運！

　　雖然前面說過遺傳的力量，我們卻不能任由基因來帶領我們一生。中國人有種說法：一命，二運，三風水，四積陰德，五讀書；我寧可相信，我們的想法決定了我們的命運。例如，父母親中若有一或二人患有糖尿病，則可教導孩子從小就注意飲食，少吃糖分高的食物和飲料、養成多運動、多休息的生活習慣。
又如，父母親若其中一人患精神病，則可自幼教導孩
子養成愉快的思緒、不計較的氣度，不但高 EQ，還
要有高 AQ（面對逆境的彈性和樂觀）……等等。

就如台大病理科醫生李豐所説的，我們快樂時，
細胞都亮亮飽飽的。我們在壓力下時，則細胞會變成
皺縮縮的，身心當然都不舒服。看到這樣的資訊，我
們還能常常愁眉苦臉嗎？笑一個吧！

第一步　看中文聽英文；若有疑問，才參考書後的英文。
（至少 2 次）🎧

第二步　眼看中文，口中隨著 CD，練習中翻英。🎧

第三步　不看中文、耳聽 CD，練習把英文翻成中文；若
有疑問，才參考書中的中文。🎧

I.V. (Intravenous)

打點滴

　　我有一個朋友前天被車撞了。他的右半身從腳到大腿還包括了整個腰部都上了石膏（但石膏在他的下腹部、生殖器部份和臀部都留有空間），而且還有內傷。他腹內的一個十分重要的器官——胰臟——被撞傷了。

　　胰臟的功能是分泌一些可以幫助消化食物的酵素

到腸子裏。胰臟另外還有一個功能，就是製造胰島素，我們所吃的食物中所轉換的血糖，就是由胰島素從血液帶到全身各組織。

我的朋友在胰臟恢復期間都不能吃東西。醫院給他打點滴，以便提供他身體所需的水分、營養和維他命。他們把一支細針刺進他手背上的靜脈。(點滴的縮寫叫做 I.V.，原文是 intravenous，表示「在靜脈內」的意思。) 我的朋友可以下床走動，但是要很小心，以防管子被拉出來。醫生護士會定時檢查他打點滴的地方有沒有被感染發炎。

第一步 看中文聽英文；若有疑問，才參考書後的英文。(至少 2 次)

第二步 眼看中文，口中隨著 CD，練習中翻英。

第三步 不看中文、耳聽 CD，練習把英文翻成中文；若有疑問，才參考書中的中文。

可使用單字

1. 點滴   I.V. (intravenous) (intra—內部的,
                    [ɪntrə`vinəs]   venous—靜脈的)

2. 石膏   cast

3. 大腿   thigh

4. 腰   waist

5. 腹部   abdomen

6. 臀部   butt (= buttocks)

7. 胰臟   pancreas

8. 酵素   enzyme

9. 胰島素   insuline

10. 靜脈	vein
11. 管子	tube
12. 感染了	infected (*adj.*)
13. 感染	infection (*n.*)
14. 住院	admitted to the hospital
15. 糖尿病	diabetes
16. 心靈溝通的坦白談話	rap session
17. 注射	injection
18. 尿液	urine
19. 少量	in moderation
20. 田徑隊	track & field team
21. 截肢	amputate

實例

41

Cosmetic Surgeries (Plastic Surgeries)

整　形

　　看到愈來愈多的人整形，我們也不妨來看看這個有趣的話題。現在的整形醫生拜豐富的科學和日益進步的技術所賜，可以讓許多男女經由各種美容手術而改頭換面。

面容整形更是普遍：整臉、拉皮、眉毛抬高、眼皮手術、脖子拉皮、消除法令紋……等等手術都進步神速，隱藏了我們年齡所帶來的老態。

於是，許多男性和女性都爲了不要打輸這場年齡之仗而去整形，因爲模樣改變了之後，外表看起來較年輕，就感覺時光似乎眞正回到了從前！

第一步　看中文聽英文；若有疑問，才參考書後的英文。（至少 2 次）🎧

第二步　眼看中文，口中隨著 CD，練習中翻英。🎧

第三步　不看中文、耳聽 CD，練習把英文翻成中文；若有疑問，才參考書中的中文。🎧

可使用單字

1.	擁抱	embrace
2.	美容的	aesthetic
3.	改頭換面	makeover
4.	步驟	procedure
5.	拉皮	face lift
6.	抬高眉毛	brow lift
7.	眼皮手術	eyelid surgery
8.	脖子拉皮	neck lift
9.	對抗	counter
10.	老化	aging

11. 佔上風　　　　　gain the upper hand

12. 真的可這麼說　　literally

Rhinoplasty (Nose Plastic Surgery) & Breast Augmentation

鼻子整形和隆乳

鼻子重塑

　　台北和上海街頭的女孩的鼻子好像都突然長高了，的確給這些地方帶來一些美麗的景象。其實，整形醫師們都認爲塑造出一個新鼻子是現在整形市場上最普遍的一個手術。雖然許多人做了鼻子整形後並不滿意，而需要再做第二或第三次手術，但是有許多的人還是勇往直前。

隆　乳

各位可否想像，現在有許多的女大學生居然爲了隆乳手術而存錢？

我們身體上有一部位會受到生理變化和老化現象極大的影響，那就是乳房！歲月、老化、地心引力、生產、餵母乳（其實這對產婦和嬰兒都最好）通常會漸漸使乳房下垂。但是我要奉勸妳們一句話：不要爲了討好男友或丈夫而隆乳，因爲一個眞正愛妳的人是不會嫌妳的！

第一步 看中文聽英文；若有疑問，才參考書後的英文。
（至少 2 次）

第二步 眼看中文，口中隨著 CD，練習中翻英。

第三步 不看中文、耳聽 CD，練習把英文翻成中文；若
有疑問，才參考書中的中文。

1. 重塑		reshape
2. 反應		reflect
3. 候選人		candidate
4. 隆乳		breast augmentation
5. 影響		impact
6. 生理		physiology
7. 老化過程		aging process
8. 地心引力		gravity
9. 生產		childbirth
10. 餵母奶		breast feeding

11. 趨勢	tendency
12. 情人眼裏出西施	Beauty is in the eye of the beholder.

43

Botox Injections

打肉毒桿菌

電視上經常可見肉毒桿菌的廣告。但是到底注射肉毒桿菌有沒有危險？有何副作用？答案是肯定的！因為即使只注射適量的劑量，手術的環境也十分衛生，大多數人仍會有輕微的副作用！

副作用可能持續一星期，包括局部無力、瘀血、腫脹、敏感……等等。大多數的人會感到肌肉變得遲

鈍，不過這只是因爲毒性進入肌肉組織之後的一個正常反應。還有極少數的人會感到說話、吞嚥或甚至呼吸困難，這時就要立刻看醫生了！

第一步　看中文聽英文；若有疑問，才參考書後的英文。（至少2次）🎧

第二步　眼看中文，口中隨著 CD，練習中翻英。🎧

第三步　不看中文、耳聽 CD，練習把英文翻成中文；若有疑問，才參考書中的中文。🎧

可使用單字

1. 肉毒桿菌   Botox

2. 副作用   side effect

3. 劑量   dosage

4. 衛生的   hygienic

5. 局部的   localized

6. 瘀血   bruise

7. 腫   swelling

8. 敏感度   sensitivity

9. 毒性   toxin

10. 肌肉組織   muscle tissue

11. 吞嚥   swallow

44

Anesthesia

麻　醉

　　我們常會忘記其實麻醉是整個手術的一部份！所以我們需要一些有關麻醉的基本知識，以免手術時可能會因無助而焦慮。

　　我們該知道些什麼呢？首先，有些人在麻醉過後可能會感到噁心想吐，不過這很快就會過去。有些人可會在手術後好幾個小時嗜睡，但這個現象也會好轉。其實這些反應都是因人而異，甚至有些人只是使用些微的鎮靜劑就會有副作用。因此，病人在手術過後一定要再觀察一段時間，這段時間一定要有經驗的護士在旁才行。

第一步　看中文聽英文；若有疑問，才參考書後的英文。（至少 2 次）

第二步　眼看中文，口中隨著 CD，練習中翻英。

第三步　不看中文、耳聽 CD，練習把英文翻成中文；若有疑問，才參考書中的中文。

可使用單字

1. 麻醉　　　　　　anesthesia
　　　　　　　　　[ænəsˋθiʒə]

2. 局部麻醉　　　　local anesthesia

3. 全身麻醉　　　　general anesthesia

4. 焦慮　　　　　　anxiety

5. 噁心　　　　　　nausea

6. 手術後的　　　　post-operative

7. 嗜睡　　　　　　lethargic
　　　　　　　　　[lɪˋθɑrdʒɪk]

8. 消失　　　　　　wear off

9. 鎮靜劑

sedative
[`sɛdətɪv]

The Skills of Negotiating

談判技巧

A： 你可以教我如何談判嗎？

B： 我盡力。首先，你要確定自己要的是什麼，不能模稜兩可。

A： 然後呢？

B： 也要找出對方個人和工作上的利益，這樣你才能在必要時刻釋出使他滿意的善意。

A： 我怎麼去發掘他們最看重的利益為何呢？

B： 一個會談判的人會問很多問題，因為在問答之中，你不但能了解到對方的立場，同時也表達了你衷心希望互惠的熱情。

A： 我是否要先發制人就能取得先機？

B： 沒這回事，讓對方先發言是個很得體的表現。

A： 如果氣氛變得不好，或是我聽到他們非善意的言論時要怎麼辦？

B： 不要在意，那不見得是針對你個人。只管鎖住議題，就事論事，就算對方言詞中懷有敵意也不要受影響。

A： 如果我節節敗退呢？

B： 休息一下，恢復精神，好像充了電一樣。但是記得回到談判桌時，要把剛才已達成的部份協議重述一次。

A： 如果談判沒有任何結果呢？

B： 沒什麼大不了的，談判的真正精神是要創造雙
贏，而不是打敗對方。只要約個時間，下一次再
談，但是再次的談判可是很傷神的，你要有所準
備才行哦！

第一步 看中文聽英文；若有疑問，才參考書後的英文。
（至少2次）

第二步 眼看中文，口中隨著 CD，練習中翻英。

第三步 不看中文、耳聽 CD，練習把英文翻成中文；若
有疑問，才參考書中的中文。

1. 認清	identify
2. 模稜兩可	waffle
3. 最主要的利益	crucial interest
4. 創造	construct
5. 吸引人的	appealing
6. 對方	the other party
7. 互惠	mutually beneficial
8. 先下手爲強	gain the upper hand by striking first
9. 良善大方的	gracious

10. 不懷好意的言詞	sarcastic remarks
11. 認為針對個人	take it personally
12. 緊鎖議題，就事論事	issue-oriented
13. 敵意	hostility
14. 節節敗退	lose ground
15. 精神一振	refreshed
16. 充電	recharged
17. 共識	consensus
18. 腦力激盪的	brainstorming
19. 雙贏的局面	a win-win situation

The Skills of Debating

辯論的技巧

A： 記得上次我提到談判的真正意義嗎？

B： 記得，創造雙贏的局面。你可以再教我一些辯論
的竅門嗎？

A： 我想一想……其實辯論沒有一定的方式，你可以
很沈穩內斂，也可以既大聲又有趣。

B： 我比較喜歡沈穩內斂的方式。

A： 那麼你說話的速度要快一點，尤其在做英語辯論時，聽起來你的頭腦才比較靈光。辯論時說話的速度夠快，也才能讓你把話說完。

B： 我在整個辯論過程中態度要如何？是否要針鋒相對？

A： 在攻擊對手的辯詞時，可以咄咄逼人，但是在表達自己的論點時，則宜冷靜沈著。記得：永遠不要耍嘴皮！

B： 如果我參加辯論比賽，應該怎麼穿著？

A： 如果全隊的人穿著一致，會讓評審潛意識替「團隊的協調性」一項加分！

B： 如果我是正方，應該如何開始？

A： 把你的議題清楚定位，並使其合理化。

B： 如果我在反方呢？

A： 對於正方的議題立場做出回應，並且明白說出它不合理的原因。

B： 又該如何結束呢？

A： 合理的、具有挑戰性的結語，會使你的辯論強有
力，並加深說服力！

B： 還有什麼是我需注意的？

A： 只要記著：一個既好又幽默的辯論者絕對勝過一
個只是「善辯」的對手。

第一步 看中文聽英文；若有疑問，才參考書後的英文。
（至少 2 次）

第二步 眼看中文，口中隨著 CD，練習中翻英。

第三步 不看中文、耳聽 CD，練習把英文翻成中文；若
有疑問，才參考書中的中文。

可使用單字

1. 竅門　　　　　　　　　tips

2. 內斂的　　　　　　　　restrained

3. 精明的　　　　　　　　shrewd

4. 機靈的　　　　　　　　resourceful

5. 針鋒相對的　　　　　　blow-for-blow

6. 積極的，咄咄逼人的　　aggressive

7. 伸展觀念　　　　　　　advance

8. 潛意識的　　　　　　　subconscious

9. 評估　　　　　　　　　assess

10. 全隊的協調度	teamwork
11. 穿著	attire (*v.t.*)
12. 形式上	in formality
13. 正方	pro side
14. 反方	con side
15. 定義	define
16. 議題	motion
17. 使之合理化	justify
18. 回應	respond
19. 說明	state

20. 具說服力的　　　　　　persuasive

21. 耍嘴皮　　　　　　　　talk glibly

47

Don't Freak out, Moms and Dads!

爸媽別抓狂！

A： 嘿！穩著點！幹嘛火冒三丈？

B： 我的兒子和女兒從不幫忙收拾房子，今天早上我還坐在一團嚼過的口香糖上面！

A： 沒什麼大不了的，你只要口氣平和而堅定地請他們把它擦掉就是了。

B： 我氣得要抓狂了。現在的年輕人真不像話！

A： 但是你知道今天的年輕人也是最不快樂的嗎？愈來愈多的人被偷襲和強暴；他們對茫茫的前途感到恐懼；還有，朋友以及傳播媒體所帶來的各種誘惑，都讓他們害怕！而我們年輕時就只需面對貧窮的問題而已！

B： 什麼誘惑？

A： 毒品、性、名牌、炫的手機……等等，這些都使他們迷失了方向！

B： 對耶！有些人甚至還因此去援交和販毒！

A： 他們真的需要我們幫助，這是父母和老師所責無旁貸的！

B： 可是他們那麼乖張，令人難以應對！

A： 你只要記得，這些正在成長的年輕人同時也是很容易受傷害的、無所適從的、無助的、焦慮的，甚至患有憂鬱症，有些還嚴重失眠呢！

B： 那我該怎麼做呢？

A： 你首先要用極大的同理心來接受他們，然後從書本或專家那裏學習智慧。給你參考一下，我個人對孩子們是軟硬兼施，賞罰分明，這個方法有效極了！

第一步 看中文聽英文；若有疑問，才參考書後的英文。（至少 2 次）🎧

第二步 眼看中文，口中隨著 CD，練習中翻英。🎧

第三步 不看中文、耳聽 CD，練習把英文翻成中文；若有疑問，才參考書中的中文。🎧

可使用單字

1. 冒煙、氣得冒煙　　　　fume

2. 收拾房子　　　　　　　pick up the room

3. 一團嚼過的口香糖　　　a wad of gum

4. 挪開，洗掉　　　　　　remove

5. 抓狂　　　　　　　　　freak out

6. 太不像樣了　　　　　　need to shape up

7. 從人的背後勒住脖子　　mugging

8. 令人毛骨悚然的　　　　appalling

9. 令人心慌的　　　　mind-boggling

10. 誘惑　　　　　　　temptation

11. 驚人的　　　　　　horrendous

12. 名牌　　　　　　　brand names

13. 炫的　　　　　　　fancy

14. 手機　　　　　　　cell phone (= mobile phone)

15. 等等　　　　　　　the list goes on

16. 迷失方向的　　　　disoriented

17. 販毒　　　　　　　traffic in narcotics

18. 援交　　　　　　　prostitute

19. 逃避責任   shirk responsibility

20. 乖張的   perverse

21. 對付   cope

22. 正在長羽毛的   fledging

23. 脆弱的   vulnerable

24. 無所適從的   maladjusted

25. 失眠   insomnia

26. 軟硬兼施   carrot-and-stick strategy

27. 給你參考一下   for your reference

You Can Run the Show, Too!

你也罩得住的！

A： 要怎麼做才能成為好老師？

B： 一個好老師不但會教、有實力、會表達，而且渾
身散發教學的熱忱、又能吸引學生全神貫注，因
為他每堂課的教學方法早就作好了計畫。

A：我已經盡力了！但有時候看到學生上課無精打采的樣子，還真令人洩氣！

B：一個好老師要在課堂上製造最佳的學習氣氛，而且所教授的課程內容都應該是實用，並有助於他們未來的工作。

A：但有些學生實在可惡，真不知要怎麼教才行！

B：你要努力地發掘出他們的優點和才華，絕不輕言放棄任何一個學生，因為每個人都有他獨特的潛能。

A：很難哦。因為我有時候就是罩不住他們。

B：只要你自己有實力，而且嚴格地管教他們，就算他們做錯事，你也願意原諒他們，你就管得住他們了。

A：我比較疼愛那些整齊又乖巧的孩子。

B：絕對不可！有些學生是被家庭犧牲了，如果連我們都不接受、不幫助他們，他們就沒希望了。永遠不要對孩子偏心！

第一步 看中文聽英文；若有疑問，才參考書後的英文。（至少 2 次）🎧

第二步 眼看中文，口中隨著 CD，練習中翻英。🎧

第三步 不看中文、耳聽 CD，練習把英文翻成中文；若有疑問，才參考書中的中文。🎧

1. 散發	exude
2. 引人注意	capture someone's attention
3. 無聊的	bored
4. 感到挫折	frustrated
5. 最佳的	optimal
6. 課堂的氣氛	classroom climate
7. 使和……相關	link...to
8. 事業	career
9. 可惡的	detestable

10. 努力追尋	seek out!
11. 優點	merit
12. 每一個（強調）	every single one of them
13. 潛力	potential
14. 罩得住，主導	run the show
15. 有實力	truly competent
16. 沒得商量	uncompromising (*adj.*)
17. 嚴格	strict
18. 疼愛	favor (*v.*)
19. 整齊	neat
20. 被犧牲	victimized
21. 偏心	play favorites

實例 49

Rise above It!

看開點兒！

A: 我覺得好煩躁。

B: 你有什麼心事？

A: 我已經有五年沒加薪了，但我真是一點辦法也沒有！看來我要去和我的上司套套交情了！

B: 你不用千方百計想升官。等你成功之時，錢自然就來了。

A: 但是我已經沒日沒夜地工作了，為什麼還沒成功？

B： 並不是辛勤工作的人就一定成功，但我也不是說
人不用努力哦！

A： 你有些自相矛盾哦！

B： 成功還需要其他的因素，包括絕對的樂觀、敏銳
的洞察力、活潑的創意、和諧的人際關係，以及
健康的身體！

A： 然後就可以過著無憂無慮的生活了？

B： 沒這回事！如果你不快樂，「成功」就不具任何意
義了。

A： 哎！你還真難纏。你到底想說什麼？

B： 這我們以後再說吧！

第一步 看中文聽英文；若有疑問，才參考書後的英文。
（至少 2 次）🎧

第二步 眼看中文，口中隨著 CD，練習中翻英。🎧

第三步 不看中文、耳聽 CD，練習把英文翻成中文；若
有疑問，才參考書中的中文。🎧

1. 煩躁   fidgety

2. 束手無策   one's hands are tied

3. 加薪   raise (*n. & v.*)

4. 不妨   might as well

5. 結交富人   get in with the rich

6. 上司   superior

7. 鑽營   go to all lengths

8. 馬不停蹄，不分日夜   around the clock

9. 品德   virtue

10. 勤奮	diligence
11. 矛盾的	contradictory
12. 樂觀	optimism
13. 尖銳、敏銳的	keen
14. 洞察力	insight
15. 生動的	vivid
16. 和諧的	harmonious
17. 人際關係	interpersonal relationship
18. 無憂無慮的	carefree
19. 彆扭的	testy
20. 你到底想說什麼？	What are you getting at?

50

Exuding Personal Magnetism!

散發個人魅力！

A： 我想做一個真正的美女。

B： 大家都想當美女。但是要內外兼具才算美。

A： 我知道外在美指的是美好的容貌。

B： 它包括個人穿衣的風格、臉孔、身材、頭髮、禮

儀（包括風度、動作和衛生習慣）、走路和坐姿、
一顰一笑、發聲，甚至面對大眾時談吐得宜。

A：簡直難以想像（有多美）！

B：但是，這些雖然重要，卻不是最重要的。

A：真的？還少了什麼嗎？

B：你如果沒有內在美，外表再怎樣漂亮也不算真
美。只有內在美可以幫助我們長久散發個人的魅
力。

A：那我要如何培養內在美呢？

B：那是一種心境，你必須把它融入你的生活當中。
然後這些內在的資質就會潛移默化，成你的外在
之美。

A：不懂。

B：你心中要有愛和自律。

A：你指的是博愛嗎？

B：正是。無私的愛使你時時喜樂、願意寬恕人、關
心人、體諒人，而且謙卑。

A：真好！還有，自律也會讓我美麗嗎？

B： 當然。自律使你穩重、可信賴、充滿自信，而且
令人尊敬。

A： 好難哦！我沒辦法全部做到！

B： 但這一切會讓你深具魅力，而魅力是一種無形而
奇妙的東西，它會使你美極了！

第一步 看中文聽英文；若有疑問，才參考書後的英文。
（至少 2 次）🎧

第二步 眼看中文，口中隨著 CD，練習中翻英。🎧

第三步 不看中文、耳聽 CD，練習把英文翻成中文；若
有疑問，才參考書中的中文。🎧

1. 散發	exude
2. 個人魅力	personal magnetism
3. 內在美	inner beauty
4. 外在美	external beauty
5. 獨特的個人品味	signature style
6. 身材	figure
7. 禮儀	etiquette
8. 舉手投足	poise
9. 衛生習慣	hygiene

0.	走路的方法	walking techniques
1.	儘管如此	nonetheless
2.	最主要的	primary
3.	心境	state of mind
4.	養成一種生活方式	cultivate a lifestyle
5.	視覺之美	visual beauty
6.	自律	self-discipline (*n.* & *v.*)
7.	博愛	altruism [`æltruɪzəm]
8.	謙卑	humble
9.	穩重	staid
20.	讓人信賴的	trustworthy

21. 無形的   intangible

22. 奇妙的   magical

Urban Space

都市土地

A：你有沒有注意到，我們城市人的戶外生活空間愈
來愈小了？

B：有啊，因為愈來愈都市化了。

A：但是如果要有城市的經濟、文化、社會、娛樂，
以及知識的活化性，城市就必須要成長！

B：一點兒沒錯！還有停車問題，那更是令人痛苦！

A：我同意。我們的政府和民間企業應該儘快拿出創新的方法來解決空間不足的問題。

B：尤其在商業精華區更是擠爆了。上次我在台北市中心停車，結果花了一個多小時才找到位子，真是太擠了！

A：城市如果沒有足夠的空間，就無法注入新生命，也無法重新使力！

B：沒有空間就沒有活力，因為它的社經機制無法發動。

A：你真是點出了問題。

第一步　看中文聽英文；若有疑問，才參考書後的英文。（至少 2 次）

第二步　眼看中文，口中隨著 CD，練習中翻英。

第三步　不看中文、耳聽 CD，練習把英文翻成中文；若有疑問，才參考書中的中文。

可使用單字

1. 密集的　　　　　　　　intense

2. 都市化　　　　　　　　urbanization

3. 公家單位　　　　　　　public authorities

4. 企業家　　　　　　　　entrepreneur

5. 壓迫　　　　　　　　　press (*v.*)

6. 大面積　　　　　　　　substantial area

7. 就這個問題而言，　　　in answer to this,

8. 結果　　　　　　　　　consequently

9. 建築師	architect
10. 創新的	innovative [ˋɪnəvetɪv]
11. 許可	approval (*n*.)
12. 保留	retain
13. 知識方面的	intellectual (*adj*.) (亦做 *n*. 用，意指知識份子)
14. 壓抑	stifle
15. 稀少的	scarce
16. 重新充滿活力	revitalization
17. 重建工作	rehabilitation

18. 有活力的	dynamic
19. 社經的	socioenonomic
20. 機制	mechanism
21. 可使用的	available
22. 促使	prompt
23. 走廊	corridor

Icebergs (I)

冰山(一)

A： 我昨晚夢見冰山了，你有沒有看過冰山？

B： 看過兩次。

A： 我只在「探索」頻道上看過，好壯觀哦！

B： 冰山真的很壯觀！

A： 冰山爲什麼是白色的？裏面是不是含有什麼物
　　質？

B：沒有，它是因爲裏面有許多的小氣泡，所以會顯
出白色來；有的冰山裏面沒有氣泡的話，就會呈
現出藍色！

A：這藍色從哪來的？

B：原理就和天空被反射成藍色一樣：都是光的作
用。我有一次在阿拉斯加還看到一整座冰山發出
藍寶石的光芒呢！

A：我眞是望塵莫及，眞希望能多旅行來拓展我的視
野。

B：可以，但也不能急。時間到了，自然就成行了。

A：原來如此。但冰山是怎麼形成的？

B：其實冰山是從冰河變來的。

A：冰河？冰河怎麼會和冰山扯上關係呢？

B：我等會兒再告訴你。

第一步　看中文聽英文；若有疑問，才參考書後的英文。（至少 2 次）🎧

第二步　眼看中文，口中隨著 CD，練習中翻英。🎧

第三步　不看中文、耳聽 CD，練習把英文翻成中文；若有疑問，才參考書中的中文。🎧

可使用單字

1. 冰山　　　　　　　　iceberg

2. 冰河　　　　　　　　glacier

3. 壯觀的　　　　　　　magnificent

4. 理所當然　　　　　　be supposed to

5. 透明的　　　　　　　transparent

6. 氣泡　　　　　　　　air bubbles

7. 上色、帶著淡淡的……　tint (*n.* & *v.*)
   色彩

8. 現象　　　　　　　　phenomenon (*pl.*
   phenomena)

9. 發光	glow
10. 藍寶石	sapphire
11. 望塵莫及	feel left in the dust
12. 開眼界	broaden one's horizons
13. 累積	accumulate
14. 滑行 (像蛇一樣爬行)	creep
15. 前進	advance
16. 可食用的	edible
17. 淡水	fresh water
18. 鹹水	seawater

Icebergs (II)

冰山(二)

A： 冰河由雪而來，它其實是千萬年的白雪堆積而成
的！

B： 然後冰河裂開，變成冰山？

A： 差不多。因為積雪很重，所以就會慢慢滑到海邊，
然後冰河的邊緣碰到海，斷裂出來，就成了冰山。

B： 我們常說「冰山之一角」，到底這一角是多大？

A：冰的密度是每立方公尺有 900 公斤的重量，海水則是每立方公尺 1,025 公斤，所以冰山比海水輕，它們是以 900 比 1,025，比例差不多是 9：10，所以約有十分之九的冰山在水面下。

B：哇！所以冰山只是全座山的 1/10？

A：對。但你知道冰山通常並不是浮在水面上，而是固定在海底的嗎？

B：好奇妙哦！

A：那我考考你一個問題：冰山鹹不鹹？

B：我想想看。

A：給你一個提示：它是白雪形成的，不是海水哦。

B：知道了！冰山根本就可以吃嘛！

第一步　看中文聽英文：若有疑問，才參考書後的英文。
　　　　（至少 2 次）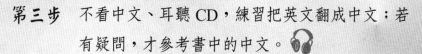

第二步　眼看中文，口中隨著 CD，練習中翻英。

第三步　不看中文、耳聽 CD，練習把英文翻成中文：若
　　　　有疑問，才參考書中的中文。

1. 冰山　　　　　　iceberg

2. 形成　　　　　　form

3. 累積　　　　　　accumulate

4. 不斷的　　　　　successive

5. 層　　　　　　　layer

6. 壓縮　　　　　　compress

7. 冰河　　　　　　glacier

8. 冰河的　　　　　glacial

9. 貼著地爬行（如冰、蛇）creep (一般爬行: crawl)

10. 滑溜溜的	viscous
11. 反射	reflect
12. 整體的	overall
13. 一抹色彩	tint (*n.*)
14. 立方公尺	cubic meter
15. 密度	density
16. 比例	ratio
17. 內部溫度	interior temperature
18. 融點	melting point
19. 退化	deterioration

20. 名稱	term
21. 平板狀	tabular
22. 磚塊狀	blocky
23. 楔子狀	wedge
24. 圓頂狀	dome
25. 尖塔狀	pinnacle
26. 船塢狀	drydock
27. 固定在地面	ground
28. 海底	seabed
29. 海潮	tidal currents
30. 淡水	fresh water

Typhoons, Floods and Mudslides

颱風、淹水和土石流

　　台灣居亞熱帶，又是海中之島，飽受颱風爲患之苦。颱風是熱帶性颶風，它的威力源自雲層和雨的力量，所以和因爲氣溫升降的威力而形成之低緯度的暴風雨不一樣：前者是熱帶性颶風，後者則是由冷鋒所造成的。

　　台灣經常有颱風，造成淹水、土石流、走山……等災害，往往造成財產的損失，甚至奪去人們的生命。最近又有一個颱風侵襲台灣北部和中部，台灣的媒體就曾報導，南投縣的信義鄉就有 4,000 位居民因爲橋斷和房屋被毀而受困於山中。

　　台北市當然也躲不掉颱風，政府當局會因爲颱風而關閉金融市場，並暫時停止上學和上班。同時，這樣的天氣也使台灣的交通網受到波及，通常國際航班仍然照常起降，但是國內的航班就常受到影響。例如，在最近一、兩次颱風中，因爲遠東航空公司有一架飛機在台北降落時滑出跑道而停飛國內線所有航班，除此之外，台北和東部之間的火車也常因颱風而停駛。

第一步　看中文聽英文；若有疑問，才參考書後的英文。（至少 2 次）🎧

第二步　眼看中文，口中隨著 CD，練習中翻英。🎧

第三步　不看中文、耳聽 CD，練習把英文翻成中文；若有疑問，才參考書中的中文。🎧

可使用單字

1. 颱風   cyclone, typhoon

2. 熱帶的   tropical

3. 起源於   derive from

4. 緯度   latitude

5. 經度   longitude

6. 溫度的升降   temperature gradient

7. 土石流   mudslide

8. 走山   landslide

9. 強力侵襲   pound

10. 政府當局	authorities
11. 干擾	disruption
12. 交通網	transport network
13. 跑道	runway
14. 暫停	suspended

The Greenhouse Effect on Earth (I)

地球的溫室效應 (一)

A： 許多人都在談溫室效應，它到底是怎麼回事？我是知道植物可以有個溫室，但它和整個地球又有什麼關連？

B： 因為我們地球的大氣層就像一幢暖房，只是暖房是把玻璃屋內的溫度加高，而大氣層是把地球加溫。我們植物的暖房是玻璃做的，一邊讓光線進來，同時卻不讓裏面的熱氣跑出去。同樣的理論，大氣層中的若干氣體發揮了像植物暖房一樣的作用！

A： 什麼氣體？

B： 二氧化碳、氧化亞氮、甲烷……，當它們碰到太陽所散發的某些輻射光的波長時，所展現的顏色是透明的！

A： 我懂了！而這些透明氣體容許太陽的能量穿過大氣層而直達地球表面。但是雲層可以阻擋光線啊！

B： 一點也沒錯！但也只有百分之三十的輻射被雲層、高山積雪以及空氣中的微小粒子反射回去。不過這也並非壞事，因爲如果沒有這個天然的阻擋者，熱能就會散到太空。地球的平均溫度就會降到攝氏零下 18 度呢！

A： 目前的平均溫度是多少？

B： 這個我們待會兒再討論。

第一步　看中文聽英文；若有疑問，才參考書後的英文。
（至少 2 次）

第二步　眼看中文，口中隨著 CD，練習中翻英。

第三步　不看中文、耳聽 CD，練習把英文翻成中文；若
有疑問，才參考書中的中文。

The Greenhouse Effect on Earth (II)

地球的溫室效應 (二)

A：你上次談到了地球的平均溫度。

B：哦，對，謝謝你提醒我！目前的平均溫度是攝氏零上 15 度。

A：天啊！那也就是說，如果沒有這些氣體，平均溫度會下降 33 度！

B：你是怎麼算的？

A：一個零下 18 度，一個零上 15 度，差了 33 度！

B：對。然而，有些科學家卻很擔心我們人類製造了太多的氣體，而這些氣體正是透明的，讓地球太熱了。

A：是啊，這就是文明所付出的代價！

第一步　看中文聽英文；若有疑問，才參考書後的英文。（至少 2 次）

第二步　眼看中文，口中隨著 CD，練習中翻英。

第三步　不看中文、耳聽 CD，練習把英文翻成中文；若有疑問，才參考書中的中文。

可使用單字

1. 溫室　　　　　　　greenhouse

2. 溫室效應　　　　　greenhouse effect

3. 行星　　　　　　　planet

4. 二氧化碳　　　　　carbon dioxide

5. 甲烷　　　　　　　methane

6. 笑氣（氧化亞氮）　laughing gas (= nitrous oxide)

7. 透明的　　　　　　transparent

8. 輻射狀的　　　　　radiant

9. 滲透　　　　　　　penetrate

10. 高山積雪	ice cap
11. 微小粒子	particles
12. 大地	land mass
13. 紅外線	infrared
14. 攝氏	Celsius
15. 美國太空總署	NASA (= National Autistic Studies Association)
16. 人造衛星	satellite

Air Pollution

空氣污染

A： 天空一片灰濛濛的！

B： 因為空氣污染很嚴重！工廠和汽車都在排放化學物和有毒的氣體。

A： 主要的污染源是什麼？

B： 有兩種：一種是無臭無味的一氧化碳，另一種是帶有臭味的二氧化氮。

A： 它們從哪兒來的？

B： 都來自於石化燃油的燃燒，汽油就是一例。

A： 還有沒有別的污染源？

B： 一些固體狀或液狀的微粒子、鉛……等等。這些物質充斥在空氣中，造成對人們的毒害。

A： 就是這些東西讓天空灰濛濛的？

B： 都市的空氣污染最明顯，肉眼就看得到，例如北京、上海、台北等大都市。許多城市因為人口快速增加，經濟也快速成長，而造成嚴重的環境污染。

第一步 看中文聽英文；若有疑問，才參考書後的英文。（至少 2 次）🎧

第二步 眼看中文，口中隨著 CD，練習中翻英。🎧

第三步 不看中文、耳聽 CD，練習把英文翻成中文；若有疑問，才參考書中的中文。🎧

1. 散發　　　　　emit

2. 化學物品　　　chemical

3. 污染源　　　　pollutant

4. 臭氧　　　　　ozone

5. 煙霧　　　　　smog

6. 阻擋　　　　　block

7. 輻射　　　　　radiation

8. 一氧化碳　　　carbon monoxide

9. 化石　　　　　fossil

10. 氮氣	nitrogen
11. 二氧化碳	carbon dioxide
12. 微粒子	particulate
13. 物質	matter
14. 硫磺	sulfur
15. 鉛	lead
16. 人口	population

58

The Ozone Layer

臭氧層

A：現在我們常聽到「臭氧層」這個名稱。科學家爲
什麼那麼在意它呢？

B：主要是因爲臭氧層就像地球的防曬油，它可以濾
掉紫外線，但它也正逐漸耗損！

A：嗯，我怕曬黑，尤其怕皮膚老化太快，所以都擦
防曬油。

B： 這就是重點！當臭氧層愈變愈薄，就會使我們過度暴露於紫外線，不但使皮膚老化，還可能會造成皮膚癌。尤其老人更需要仔細保護皮膚，不要受到陽光的傷害，才不容易有皺紋或是因爲光化作用而造成的厚角質，也可避免得皮膚癌。

A： 黑色素呢？我聽說亞洲人因爲黑色素比白種人多，所以皮膚較不易受到日照的傷害。

B： 你指的是「皮膚的黑色素」？我們真的比白種人幸運，因爲我們的黑色素較多，有助於抵抗光線所帶來的老化。不過醫生還是強調要塗抹防曬品，尤其皮膚特別白皙的人更容易受到陽光的傷害。

第一步　看中文聽英文；若有疑問，才參考書後的英文。（至少 2 次）🎧

第二步　眼看中文，口中隨著 CD，練習中翻英。🎧

第三步　不看中文、耳聽 CD，練習把英文翻成中文；若有疑問，才參考書中的中文。🎧

1. 防曬劑	sunblock
2. 過濾	filter
3. 紫外線	ultra-violet ray
4. 過量的	excessive
5. 老化	age
6. 免疫力	immune system
7. 收成	yield
8. 浮游植物	phytoplankton (phyto-: 植物——)

9. 光化作用的	actinic
10. 角質纖維化	keratoses

Teenagers, Parents and Schools

孩子、父母和學校

A： 我實在想不通，照理說，等學生到達高中的時候，
父母和子女之間對於孩子的學習起碼已經有十五
年的溝通，但爲什麼反而是上了高中的孩子最容
易迷失，也最叛逆？

B：這是父母、社會以及學校的共同責任，尤其是父母責無旁貸！

A：現在的年輕人接收了各種資訊，卻缺乏判斷力；身處國際村，卻缺乏宏觀；感情豐富，卻缺乏高 EQ 和高 AQ。

B：我知道 EQ 是「情緒指數」，但 AQ 是什麼？

A：AQ 是「逆境指數」。

B：那也是很重要的！父母不能把孩子的行為和學習都推給學校。

A：我同意。「沒有問題孩子，只有問題父母」，父母是孩子從小到大所看到的最佳榜樣。

B：又以上大學為例，堅強、有自信的學生通常可以根據對自我的認知和手邊的資料來決定要上哪一所大學或什麼科系，但不是所有的高中生都能如此，大多數的孩子還是很徬徨的。

A：持平而論，並不是所有的父母都知道該如何去幫助孩子。我個人認為老師可以勸家長多應參與學生的事情。

B： 怎麼說？

A： 國中和高中的老師不但有責任去和父母溝通，要
去了解學生的家庭，學校也應該有能力舉辦一些
活動，讓家庭也能夠參與孩子的學習成長、戀愛，
以及如何選擇大學科系的方向。

第一步　看中文聽英文；若有疑問，才參考書後的英文。
（至少 2 次）

第二步　眼看中文，口中隨著 CD，練習中翻英。

第三步　不看中文、耳聽 CD，練習把英文翻成中文；若
有疑問，才參考書中的中文。

1. 教育家　　　　　　educator

2. 影響、牽扯　　　　involvement

3. 能力　　　　　　　capacity

4. 執行　　　　　　　conduct

實例

60

US-China-Taiwan Relations

美-中-台關係

A： 你認為，如果台灣受到武力攻擊的話，美國會不
會出兵保護？

B： 你沒有注意到美國不斷重申它的一中政策？

A： 什麼是「一中政策」？

B： 只承認台灣是中國的一部份，而且不會支持台獨，也不希望台灣採取任何類似改變現狀的動作。

A： 爲什麼呢？

B： 因爲美國並不希望看到台灣和大陸統一之後，成爲一個強國，而同時美國認爲中國是亞洲及全球的一個不可忽視的重要勢力和戰略地位，因此它又希望和中共建立友好關係。

A： 美國也希望台灣向它買武器。

B： 另外，美國也視中共爲改善美國與北韓關係的關鍵人物。

A： 所以它不能得罪中共。

B： 對，不過中國內部也正面臨許多棘手的問題，例如宗教自由、美國所提出的軍備問題、人權、以及經濟成長……等問題。

第一步 看中文聽英文；若有疑問，才參考書後的英文。
（至少 2 次）🎧

第二步 眼看中文，口中隨著 CD，練習中翻英。🎧

第三步 不看中文、耳聽 CD，練習把英文翻成中文；若有疑問，才參考書中的中文。🎧

可使用單字

1. 現狀	status quo
2. 一中政策	One-China policy
3. 台灣關係法	Taiwan Relations Act
4. 統一	reunification (*v.* reunify)
5. 事實上已爲獨立	de-facto independence
6. 提升軍備	weapons proliferation
7. 平壤	Pyongyang (常代表北韓)

Taiwan (I)— Its History

台灣 (一)——歷史

A： 台灣爲什麼也叫做「福爾摩沙」？

B： 那是「可愛」的意思，是葡萄牙佔領台灣時所取
的名字。

A： 真的？好可愛的名字！

B： 但是台灣這個「美麗之島」卻有著滄桑的歷史。

A： 怎麼說？台灣有段傷心的往事嗎？

---

* 一般狀況下，台灣應該用 "she" 表示其美麗迷人之意，但這一章因
為在述說台灣的歷史，所以用 "Its History" 比 "Her History" 恰
當。

279

B： 在 1895 年的甲午戰爭之後，中國和日本簽訂「馬關條約」把台灣割讓給日本。台灣人在日本的統治之下吃了許多苦。

A： 難怪我一個朋友的媽媽現在還會說日文。但台灣後來不是在第二次世界大戰之後就歸還中國了嗎？

B： 是歸還了，但是中國共產黨打敗國民黨之後，國民黨就帶著 200 萬人逃到台灣。

A： 然後又發生了 228 事件？

B： 對，在 1947 年。許多台灣人和外省人都在那次事件中遇害。

A： 往好處想，在之後的五十多年間，執政者逐漸使台灣民主化，並使納入政府的體制之內。

B： 其實，台灣在已逝的蔣經國先生帶領之下，逐漸走向民主，台灣也從貧窮變繁榮，甚且成為亞洲四小龍之一。

A： 而且在西元 2000 年，台灣第一次政黨輪替，從國民黨換成民進黨執政。

B： 的確如此。

第一步　看中文聽英文；若有疑問，才參考書後的英文。
（至少 2 次）

第二步　眼看中文，口中隨著 CD，練習中翻英。

第三步　不看中文、耳聽 CD，練習把英文翻成中文；若
有疑問，才參考書中的中文。

可使用單字

1. 甲午戰爭   Jiawu War (*or* Nisshin War)

2. 馬關條約   Treaty of Shimonoseki

3. 割讓   cede

4. 回歸   revert

5. 國民黨員   Nationalist

6. 憲法   constitution

7. 十年   decade

8. 使民主化   democratize

9. 使……結合 incorporate

10. 進行	undergo
11. 政權轉換	transfer of power
12. 民進黨	Democratic Progressive Party (= DPP)
13. 國民黨	Kuomintang (= KMT) 或 Nationalist Party
14. 亞洲四小龍	East Asia's Four Economic "Tigers"
15. 親民黨	People First Party (= PFP)
16. 台聯黨	Taiwan Solidarity Union (= TSU)
17. 新黨	Chiness New Party (= CNP)

Taiwan (II)—Its Politics

台灣（二）——政治

A：台灣有幾個政黨？

B：目前有五個主要政黨，包括民進黨、國民黨、親民黨、台聯黨、新黨。

A：其中，民進黨和台聯黨都反對台灣和大陸統一。

B：對。而反對台灣獨立者則希望大陸慢慢經由民主和經濟的自然演變，並和台灣再和平相處個 50 年再說，以免台灣淪為戰場。

A： 台灣的國際關係似乎十分複雜。舉例來說，西沙群島目前由大陸管理，但是台灣說那是屬於他們的。還有釣魚台也是個問題，又如台灣說釣魚台是他們的，但是目前卻由日本管轄。

B： 對，媒體的報導以及民間的抗議更凸顯了這些事情。

第一步　看中文聽英文；若有疑問，才參考書後的英文。（至少 2 次）🎧

第二步　眼看中文，口中隨著 CD，練習中翻英。🎧

第三步　不看中文、耳聽 CD，練習把英文翻成中文；若有疑問，才參考書中的中文。🎧

可使用單字

1. 辯論、爭議   debate

2. 主流   mainstream

3. 國內政治   domestic politics

4. 政治開方   political liberalization

5. 立法院   legislature

6. 國家認同   national identity

7. 共識   consensus

8. 事實   de facto

9. 最後結果	ultimate outcome
10. 主張	advocate
11. 立場	stand
12. 主權國	sovereign nation
13. 世台會	World United Formosans for Independence
14. 汶萊	Brunei
15. 南沙群島	Spratly Islands
16. 欠缺	fall short of
17. 具法律的約束力	legally binding

18. 西沙群島	Paracel Islands
19. 釣魚台	Senkaku Islands (日本方面的說法) Diaoyu Tai (中、台的說法)
20. 媒體報導	media coverage

其他重要單字：

1. 年齡層	age bracket
2. 壽命	life expectancy
3. 族群	ethnic group
4. 客家人	Hakka

5. 外省人	mainland Chinese
6. 原住民	aborigine
7. 政黨	political party
8. 有活力的	dynamic
9. 政府當局	government authorities
10. 趨勢	trend
11. 工業機構	industrial firm
12. 民營化	privatize
13. 原動力	impetus
14. 工業化	industrialization

15. 貿易順差	trade surplus
16. 外匯存底	foreign reserves
17. 追上	overtake
18. 景氣沈滯不前	downturn
19. 呆帳	bad debt
20. 脆弱的	fragile; vulnerable

How Arabs See America (I) (The Cons)

阿拉伯人看美國(一) (反對者的看法)

A： 我真的很同情伊拉克。兩個西方大國帶軍隊到那裏去打仗，好好一個國家變成了殺戮戰場。

B： 他們人民很痛苦，其實許多阿拉伯人心中所求所想的就是能夠過點兒好日子。

A： 而唯一有能力幫助他們解決中東的種族和宗教衝突的國家就是美國，但這個世界警察卻在中東引發了更多的流血！

B： 我有一次在新聞上聽到阿拉伯人民說，如果美國真的有心願意協調區域性的解除武裝和維持安定，他們是很願意去配合的！但是他們卻感到非常焦慮、失望和憤怒！

A： 我可以體會他們的感受。他們覺得美國所重視的是油田的利益，而非阿拉伯人的福祉。

B： 現在整個中東地區的反美情緒十分高漲！

A： 而這種仇恨在伊斯蘭教的基本教義派中更是強烈。一個著名的伊斯蘭教的牧者在阿拉伯最大的清真寺講道時，沈痛地告訴他的教友：美國要的就是兩樣：石油，還有就是爲了它自己的利益而幫助以色列。

第一步　看中文聽英文；若有疑問，才參考書後的英文。
（至少 2 次）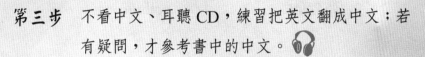

第二步　眼看中文，口中隨著 CD，練習中翻英。

第三步　不看中文、耳聽 CD，練習把英文翻成中文；若
有疑問，才參考書中的中文。

1. 種族的	ethnic
2. 處理	tackle
3. 巴勒斯坦	Palestinian
4. 燃起火花	spark (*n.* & *v.*)
5. 戰線	front
6. 不安定	instability
7. 撤武	disarmament (*n.*) (*v.* disarm)
8. 政權	regime

9. 巴格達　　　　　　Baghdad (伊拉克首府，所以常
　　　　　　　　　　　代表伊拉克)

10. 基本教義派　　　　fundamentalist

11. 信奉伊斯蘭教的團體　Islamic circle

12. 盟友　　　　　　　ally

13. 陰謀　　　　　　　conspiracy

14. 講道　　　　　　　sermon

15. 清真寺　　　　　　mosque

64

How Arabs See America (II)
(The Pros)

阿拉伯人看美國 (二)
(支持者的看法)

A： 但是仍然有一些沈默的極少數人同情美國在這個
地方的策略。

B： 他們的觀點如何？

A： 他們感激美國，因爲當全世界都不能管、也不想管他國內部事務的時候，美國卻秉持著勇氣和正義扮起了世界警察。

B： 所以他們期待美國和英國爲他們維護國際和平與規範？

A： 是啊。他們就十分讚賞美國出兵干預當時阿富汗的塔里班政權一事。目前的回教國家太弱、太亂，尚無任何能力來處理類似的問題，他們認爲在這種情況下，也只有讓像美國這種國家來處理了。

B： 但是，不管正方和反方都一致認爲美國應該用和平的外交手法來進行，例如用談判的方式來解決。

A： 但是美國和英國卻用轟炸來處理問題，製造了新敵人，才引發賓拉登這種人物出現。

B： 賓拉登一直有許多的追隨者哦！

A： 總之，我的想法是，中東亟望見到一個公平的撤武政策。

B： 那以色列也該一起撤武嘍！

第一步 看中文聽英文：若有疑問，才參考書後的英文。
（至少 2 次）🎧

第二步 眼看中文，口中隨著 CD，練習中翻英。🎧

第三步 不看中文、耳聽 CD，練習把英文翻成中文；若
有疑問，才參考書中的中文。🎧

1. 存疑的　　　　　　　skeptical

2. 沒聲音的　　　　　　muted

3. 同情　　　　　　　　sympathize (+ with)

4. 干預　　　　　　　　intervention (*v.* intervene)

5. 足夠的立場　　　　　solid ground

6. 嗤之以鼻　　　　　　flout

7. 不干預　　　　　　　nonintervention

8. 內政　　　　　　　　internal matters

9. 波西尼亞　　　　　　Bosnia

10. 科索渥	Kosovo
11. 規範	norm
12. 阿富汗	Afghanistan
13. 塔里班政權	Taliban regime
14. 掃除恐怖主義	eliminate terrorism
15. 外交管道	diplomatic means
16. 徵召新手	recruit
17. 公平公正	even-handed
18. 海珊	Saddam Hussein
19. 在國與國之間	across the board

20. 以色列人　　　　　　Israelis

Al Jazeera

半島電視台

A： 你有沒有聽過「半島電視台」？

B： 有啊。那是一家中東地區非常有名的電視台。它曾經播放美軍和英軍虐待伊拉克戰俘，以及美國人質被伊拉克民兵斬首的錄影帶。怎麼啦？

A： 伊拉克的行政院長最近命令暫時關閉半島電視台在首府巴格達的辦事處。

B：眞的？但是半島電視台向數百萬的阿拉伯人播放消息，而且因爲它所報導的地區往往太危險，也只有它肯去一般西方的媒體工作者認爲太危險而不敢去的地方！它爲什麼被關閉？

A：嗯，伊拉克新政府所持的理由是半島電視台干擾了當地的安全，所以必須暫時關閉。

B：眞可惜！半島電視台爲整個阿拉伯世界提供了有關伊拉克消息的主要管道，而且新政府違背了它曾經說過將帶給伊拉克人民一個「新生命，以及擁有言論自由和民主開放的新紀元」的承諾。

A：因爲美國認爲半島電視台會鼓吹民兵，而且美國政府對它的不滿是由來已久，美國一直認爲它經常播放對美國不友善的消息。

第一步 看中文聽英文：若有疑問，才參考書後的英文。
（至少 2 次）🎧

第二步 眼看中文，口中隨著 CD，練習中翻英。🎧

第三步 不看中文、耳聽 CD，練習把英文翻成中文；若有疑問，才參考書中的中文。🎧

可使用單字

1. 行政院長	prime minster
2. 半島電視台	AI Jazeera
3. 主要來源	primary source
4. 大幅度的報導	extensive coverage
5. 民兵	militant
6. 布希政府	Bush administration
7. 有偏見的	biased
8. 引用	cite
9. 錄影帶	videotape

10. 斬首	behead
11. 人質	hostage
12. 網站	Web site
13. 沒道理	unjustified
14. 誓言	pledge
15. 新紀元	new era

US vs. NK (US Stance)

美國 vs. 北韓

(美國的立場)

A： 為什麼美國和北韓好些年的談判並沒有得到任何
實質上的結論？

B： 因為美國和北韓在基本態度上有所差異。

A： 我知道美國要求北韓立刻拆除所有的核武裝備。

B：對，完全拆除、沒有商榷的餘地，還要能夠證實這些設備已完全拆除，並且不能再使用。

A：但是北韓為什麼要聽話呢？他們有沒有提出什麼要求？

B：雖然美國堅持它的立場要北韓放棄核武，但是它並沒有對北韓做出任何具體的提案。除此之外，美國也強調北韓的傳統武器、生化武器、人權以及許多其他事項都需要做重新評估和適度的調整。

A：美國致力於維持亞洲的和平。

B：某方面而言，的確如此。但是一個強大的亞洲核武國家對美國的全球性戰略而言，是一個威脅。

第一步　看中文聽英文；若有疑問，才參考書後的英文。（至少 2 次）🎧

第二步　眼看中文，口中隨著 CD，練習中翻英。🎧

第三步　不看中文、耳聽 CD，練習把英文翻成中文；若有疑問，才參考書中的中文。🎧

1. 拆除　　　　　　　　dismantle

2. 鈽元素 (Pu)　　　　　plutonium

3. 鈾元素 (U)　　　　　uranium

4. 可以被證實的　　　　verifiable

5. 不能再使用的　　　　irreversible

6. 再三聲明　　　　　　assert

7. 使關係正常化　　　　normalize

8. 飛彈　　　　　　　　missile

9. 傳統的　　　　　　　　conventional

10. 生化武器　　　　　　　biochemical weapon

實 例

67

NK vs. US (NK's Stance)

北韓 vs. 美國

(北韓的立場)

A： 目前北韓對美國的提議有何反應呢？

B： 他們當然不喜歡美國那種一意孤行要完全消除北韓的核子防備力量的高姿態，北韓所提供的方案是「在公平和有彈性的原則之下，展開配套行動。」

A：他們希望能符合雙方和利益？

B：是的。北韓希望凍結的核子設備僅限於核子武器，並不包括用於和平措施所使用的核能裝備。他們希望美國能有善意的回應。

A：那也合理啊！他們要求什麼善意的回應呢？

B：他們要求美國將北韓從主導恐怖活動的名單中移除、提供石油和電力、並鬆綁美國對北韓的政治和經濟的制裁與封鎖。

A：但是我以為北韓否認它擁有鈾核武。

B：它是否認，它說美國的指控是無的放矢。不過它在 2005 年終於承認它的確擁有核武。

第一步 看中文聽英文；若有疑問，才參考書後的英文。（至少 2 次）🎧

第二步 眼看中文，口中隨著 CD，練習中翻英。🎧

第三步 不看中文、耳聽 CD，練習把英文翻成中文；若有疑問，才參考書中的中文。🎧

可使用單字

1. 放棄　　　　　abandon

2. 具體的　　　　concrete

3. 提案　　　　　proposal

4. 協調　　　　　coordinate

5. 平壤　　　　　Pyongyang

6. 方法　　　　　measures

7. 配套　　　　　package

8. 同步的　　　　simultaneous

9. 含鈾元素的　　uranium-enriched

10. 指控	accusation
11. 毫無根據的	groudless
12. 消除	eliminate
13. 遏阻的	deterrent
14. 壓抑	stifle
15. 回報	inreturn for
16. 恐怖主義	terrorism
17. 柴油	fuel oil
18. 侷限	confine
19. 撇開	exempt

20. 對抗的	confrontational
21. 立場	stance
22. 平行的	parallel

About Russia—
A "Welfare" Policy

俄羅斯的「福利」法案

A： 俄羅斯總統普丁說他第二任內的主要政策是要提昇國內數百萬窮人的生活水準。他的承諾兌現了嗎？

B： 要怎麼說呢？最近俄羅斯上議院通過了一項社會改革法案，這個法案被批評和他的承諾完全背道而馳！

A： 這項法案的內容是什麼？

B： 政府將終結一連串老人及殘障者福利，包括交通和醫護免費……。

A： 他們為什麼要讓這項法案通過呢？

B： 這些議員其實只是俄羅斯政府的橡皮圖章而已，當這項法案表決時，在俄國的 179 個國會成員中，有 156 人贊成這個立法，1 人棄權。

A： 政府又為什麼要刪除這項自蘇聯時期就存在的，而且是俄羅斯最弱勢的人所仰賴的福利呢？

B： 誰知道？但我知道有一群年輕人還為此進行絕食抗議。

A： 俄羅斯窮人、殘障、老人以及第二次世界大戰的退伍軍人都將深受波及——但他們小百老姓又能對那些政客怎樣呢？

第一步　看中文聽英文；若有疑問，才參考書後的英文。
（至少 2 次）🎧

第二步　眼看中文，口中隨著 CD，練習中翻英。🎧

第三步　不看中文、耳聽 CD，練習把英文翻成中文；若
有疑問，才參考書中的中文。🎧

可使用單字

1. 上議院	upper house of parliament (美國用 senate)
2. 改革	reform
3. 法案	bill
4. 具爭議的	controversial
5. 一連串的	an array of
6. 蘇聯時期的	Soviet-era
7. 老人	elderly
8. 殘障	disabled

9. 交通	transportation
10. 方法	measure
11. 行之有年	long-standing
12. 聯邦	federation
13. 國會	council
14. 橡皮圖章	rubber-stamp
15. 立法	legislation
16. 俄國	Russia (有時用 Kremlin 代替)
17. 棄權	abstention
18. 俄國總統普丁	Vladimir Putin

19. 窮國的	inpoverished
20. 可憐的、脆弱的	vulnerable
21. 退伍軍人	veteran
22. 激起火花	spark
23. 抗議者	protestent
24. 蘇聯 (已解體)	U.S.S.R.
25. 絕食抗議	hunger strike
26. 針對的	targeted
27. 片段	segment

69

Major Economic Policies on Mainland China (I)

中國大陸的重要經濟政策 (一)

A： 中國大陸在鐵幕開啓之後，已經變成全世界最大的開發中國家。

B： 的確如此。自從中國大陸改革及開放之後，它的
政府從許多各種複雜的以及突發的狀況中學到了
經驗。

A： 大陸人多地廣、資源富饒，深具開發的潛力。

B： 你說得對。想想13億人口代表了一個多麼廣大的
市場！

A： 大陸的加工業表現地十分亮麗，因為它的勞工便
宜、人民勤奮、頭腦靈活，我認為全球的加工業
重心終將轉移到大陸。

B： 你認為中國大陸長期的經濟成長能夠成功地實現
嗎？大陸可以不再以傳統密集勞工的工業為主，
而以豐富的資金以及技術取代，來提昇經濟的發
展？

A： 我絕對相信，因為它所採取的幾個重大突破將足
以使它的經濟完全改觀。

B： 哪些突破？

A： 我待會兒再告訴你。

第一步 看中文聽英文；若有疑問，才參考書後的英文。（至少 2 次）

第二步 眼看中文，口中隨著 CD，練習中翻英。

第三步 不看中文、耳聽 CD，練習把英文翻成中文；若有疑問，才參考書中的中文。

1. 鐵幕	bamboo curtain
2. 開發中國家	developing country
3. 未開發國家	underdeveloped country
4. 已開發國家	developed country
5. 對付……問題	cope with
6. 改革	reform
7. 據說	alledgedly
8. 比較起來	comparatively
9. 加工業	processing industry
10. 容納	accommodate

1. 勞力密集工作 （例如製衣、鞋）	labor-intensive industry
2. 脫胎換骨	transformation
3. 令人難以抗拒	irresistible
4. 突破	breakthrough (*n.*)
5. 突破	break through (*v.*)

Major Economic Policies on Mainland China (II)

中國大陸的重要經濟政策 (二)

A： 我知道中國大陸的整個機構機制必須徹底改變，
尤其是政府的運作方式。

B：對。中國大陸的政府對經濟的干預已經鬆綁、並大幅提昇國內外的投資環境、交通以及法律限制等等，非常有力地激勵海內外的投資市場……等等。

A：國營企業呢？這些機構以往都壟斷了市場。

B：不再是了。國營企業的重心已經從干預轉移到協助開發境內各種事業了。

A：你是說中國大陸是毫無保留、竭盡所能來發展經濟？

B：也不能完全這麼說。但大陸的確是從頭到腳、由裏到外，上下一致來發展一個配套完整的且持續成長的經濟。

A：所以，中國大陸以前的觀念只是一味追求提昇國內生產毛額，現在則完全改觀了。

第一步 看中文聽英文；若有疑問，才參考書後的英文。（至少 2 次）🎧

第二步 眼看中文，口中隨著 CD，練習中翻英。🎧

第三步 不看中文、耳聽 CD，練習把英文翻成中文；若有疑問，才參考書中的中文。🎧

可使用單字

1. 指示	disclose
2. 人民消費	GDP
3. 超過	exceed
4. 國力	national strength
5. 逆境的	adverse
6. 壞的影響	adverse impact
7. 重回	resume
8. SARS 之前	Pre-SARS

9. 外匯存底	foreign exchange reserves
10. 城市的	urban
11. 鄉村的	rural
12. 佔高位	top (*v.*)
13. 超越	surpass
14. 三峽水壩工程	the Three Gorges water conservancy project
15. 整體經濟	aggregate economy

An Appreciation of Renminbi Yuan

人民幣升值

A： 你知道昨晚人民幣升值2.1%？

B： 知道啊，北京長期以來一直不願將人民幣升值，
昨晚突然地宣佈，還令人有些訝異！

A： 不過，這也不是人民幣第一次升值。早在 1994 和

2002 年間，它對美元的匯值就升值了 18.5％。

B： 人民幣有沒有貶值過？

A： 有。1994 年的時候就貶到 1986 年的一半。後來因爲大陸經濟起飛，所以又升值了，人民幣上上下下就像坐雲霄飛車一樣。

B： 你覺得人民幣還會漲嗎？

A： 應該會。2.1％ 只是初步的調升。中國已經決定採用以若干貨幣爲基準的、可控管的浮動匯率機制，也就是「一籃子貨幣」理論。換句話說，以後人民幣之價位將以市場爲導向。

B： 也就是説人民幣將採彈性匯率嘍。那我想我應該可以還有些賺頭！

第一步　看中文聽英文；若有疑問，才參考書後的英文。（至少 2 次）

第二步　眼看中文，口中隨著 CD，練習中翻英。

第三步　不看中文、耳聽 CD，練習把英文翻成中文；若有疑問，才參考書中的中文。

實 例

72

Zhejiang—One of the Richest Provinces in China

浙江——富裕的一省

A： 我先生升官了，但是他要被外調到他們的浙江分公司去工作。

B： 浙江？那是個好地方！我從報上看到，僅浙江一省就獨佔全中國進出口的一半以上，是個很富裕的省份！

A：但是我並不很在意這個，我只擔心孩子的就學問題。

B：這你完全不用擔心。浙江有許多好學校。何況，一家團聚才是最重要的。

A：為什麼浙江的成長這麼迅速？上次我去旅遊的時候，那地方看起來還很落後呢！

B：那是因為他們採取了「進軍全球」的目標。整個省的決策核心不只是官員，還包括了各種型態的生意人和私人公司。

A：他們採取「進軍全球」，而台灣採取「本土化」……

B：預期效果不言而喻。

第一步　看中文聽英文；若有疑問，才參考書後的英文。（至少 2 次）🎧

第二步　眼看中文，口中隨著 CD，練習中翻英。🎧

第三步　不看中文、耳聽 CD，練習把英文翻成中文；若有疑問，才參考書中的中文。🎧

可使用單字

1. 海關　　　　custom's house

2. 統計數字　　statistics

3. 外資生意　　foreign-invested

4. 企業　　　　enterprise

5. 十億　　　　billion

6. 成長率　　　growth rate

7. 比例　　　　proportion

8. 策略　　　　strategy

9. 特色　　　　feature (*n.* & *v.*)

10. 共存　　　coexist

11. 核心	core
12. 貿易商	trading form
13. 強烈的	keen
14. 每年	annual
15. 成立	implement

Taiwanese Investments in China

台商投資中國大陸

A：台商赴中國大陸投資的人口一直在增加。

B：在今年的一月至七月這半年間，有將近 1400 家公司行號申請赴中國大陸投資，這個數字比去年同時期高出了 21%。

A： 這段時期的投資總額是多少？

B： 所核准的總投資額就達 38 億美元，較去年同時期高出一半之多。

A： 高出一半？那可是個大數目！他們到哪些地方去投資？都投資哪些項目呢？

B： 這些投資大多集中於上海、廣東和浙江。至於投資的項目，主要是電子及電器產品、基本金屬製造業、塑膠製造業、化學產品製造業以及交通工具製造業。

A： 聽說許多美國的網路公司都已登陸中國大陸。

B： 對，不是經由公司合併，就是把整個公司買下來！

第一步 看中文聽英文；若有疑問，才參考書後的英文。（至少 2 次）🎧

第二步 眼看中文，口中隨著 CD，練習中翻英。🎧

第三步 不看中文、耳聽 CD，練習把英文翻成中文；若有疑問，才參考書中的中文。🎧

1. 比較起來   comparatively

2. 分配   distribution

3. 家電   electrical appliance

4. 交通工具   transportation vehicle

Singapore — A Quick Look

新加坡簡介

A： 爲什麼大多數的新加坡人會說英語？

B： 因爲新加坡早在 1819 年就成爲英屬的商業殖民地。

A： 她現在還是英國的殖民地嗎？

B： 她在 1963 年加入馬來西亞聯邦之後，就不是了。

A：難怪他們在諸族群當中，還包括了馬來人。

B：對。今天在新加坡到處都還聽到馬來語呢。

A：但是新加坡現在是獨立的城邦了。

B：城邦？那她一定比一般國家小嘍？

A：很小。她的全部面積才 693 平方公里，而台灣為 3 萬 6 千平方公里，這樣你就不難想像她有多小了。

B：不過，因為她曾是英國的商業殖民地，而且這個國家的領導人非常睿智，所以今天新加坡是全世界經濟最繁榮的國家之一。

A：沒錯。她的港口是全世界吞吐量最大的港口之一。

B：而且她的人民生產毛額等同西歐等最先進的國家！

A：那麼棒！所以她的雄厚的貿商關係、明智且具彈性的外交政策，以及勤奮的人民促成了今天富裕的新加坡！

B：不幸的是，她也無法避免工業污染以及因為土地過於狹小而帶來的垃圾處理問題。

A： 是啊。有一次印尼的森林大火還造成新加坡的天
空一片灰濛濛的！

第一步 看中文聽英文；若有疑問，才參考書後的英文。
（至少 2 次）

第二步 眼看中文，口中隨著 CD，練習中翻英。

第三步 不看中文、耳聽 CD，練習把英文翻成中文；若
有疑問，才參考書中的中文。

可使用單字

1. 殖民地	colony	
2. 隨後	subsequently	
3. 面積	area	
4. 淡水	fresh water	
5. 海水	sea water	
6. 可用上的	available	
7. 垃圾處理	garbage disposal	
8. 平均年齡	median age	
9. 族群	ethnic groups	
10. 預估	forecast predict	

11. 經濟起飛	pickup
12. 分成兩半	half
13. 觀光業	tourism
14. 全面性的	across the board
15. 展望	outlook
16. 復甦	rebound
17. 和……符合一致	in line with

75

The Depreciation Of the American Dollar

美元貶值

A： 天啊，美元在過去十年之中跌了 30%！

B： 其實那是他們刻意安排的。

A： 怎麼說？強勢貨幣不就代表國家的購買力很強嗎？

B： 不盡然。美元的強勢幣值已經使美國在出口方面喪失競爭力，同時也使美國的跨國大企業在海外所賺的利潤降低。

A： 不懂。

B： 美國公司在海外所賺的錢都是當地貨幣，對不對？

A： 對！

B： 那麼對他們的跨國企業而言，他們比較喜歡把在當地的錢換成較多還是較少的美元？

A： 哦，懂了！所以強勢的美金會降低他們的利潤！

B： 懂了吧！還有，美國每天需要由海外匯入巨額的美元，才能平衡她每天所需支付的金額差距。也就是說，美元走軟才較符合美國的利益。

A： 你懂的還真多呢！

第一步　看中文聽英文；若有疑問，才參考書後的英文。
（至少 2 次）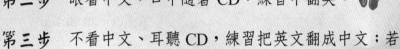

第二步　眼看中文，口中隨著 CD，練習中翻英。

第三步　不看中文、耳聽 CD，練習把英文翻成中文；若
有疑問，才參考書中的中文。

1.	美元	American dollar
2.	壓抑	depress
3.	數額	figure
4.	多國公司	multinational company
5.	跨國企業	transnational conglomerate
6.	激起	boost
7.	湧入	inflow
8.	資本	capital
9.	赤字	deficit
10.	不平衡	disequilibrium

76

World Economy

世界經濟

A：你有沒有注意到，全球經濟在過去五年下滑了？

B：當然注意到了。主要是因爲 PPP 衰落了。

A："PPP" 好像在哪裏聽過。那是什麼？

B：「國家購買力」，記得嗎？美、中、印度、日本是全球四大消費國。

A：不過全球經濟衰退已經使得許多高額的消費者走向破產一途。

B：還好，1990 年代託美國股票大漲之福，許多美國人今天仍能保有相當的財力！

A：那全球就業市場又如何呢？

B：比原先預期的表現還要好，自從 2000 年以來，終於有一點抬頭的機會了。

A：不過我知道有許多人借了錢卻還不了，因而負債累累！

第一步　看中文聽英文；若有疑問，才參考書後的英文。（至少 2 次）

第二步　眼看中文，口中隨著 CD，練習中翻英。

第三步　不看中文、耳聽 CD，練習把英文翻成中文；若有疑問，才參考書中的中文。

可使用單字

1. 軌道   track

2. 多虧   thanks to

3. 購買力等級 (PPP)   purchasing power parity

4. 國際貨幣基金會   International Monetary Foundation (= IMF)

5. 法權力   leverage

6. 破產   bankruptcy

7. 股市   stock market

Japan — The Bubble Economy

日本──泡沫經濟

A： 我們在世界各處都能見到日本的觀光客。

B： 以前是常看到，不過現在日本觀光客愈來愈少了。

A： 怎麼回事？

B： 因爲泡沫經濟破滅了。

A： 泡沫經濟是什麼東西？

B： 那是一種惡性循環。當一個貨品因爲投資客的炒作而價錢大漲的時候，更多的投資客就進來了。很快的，價錢就會漲的離譜，終於突然在一夕之間又掉了下來，就像一顆水珠掉入水中一樣，所以被稱爲「泡沫經濟」。

A： 就像「崩盤」一樣？

B： 就是崩盤！其實，日本的經濟學家最近就提出了警告，說日本的銀行呆帳已近乎全國人民消費總額的一半！

A： 天啊，那還眞糟糕啊！

B： 日本因爲工業化，而且是自由市場經濟，所以 PPP 原先佔全球第三，僅次於美國和中國大陸。

A： PPP 是什麼？

B： 就是國家購買力啊！最近因爲印度崛起，除了次於美國和大陸之外，日本的 PPP 已經落到第四了。而日本因爲經濟停滯不進，使銀行新的呆帳成長的速度相當於舊有呆帳償還的速度！

A： 日本政府難道沒有採取對策嗎？

B： 有啊，但是美國的美元政策把她壓的喘不過氣來。

A： 爲什麼？

B： 因爲美元走貶使得日圓升值。可是日本也和美國一樣，需要日幣貶值才能刺激她的經濟啊！

A： 那麼，日本經濟是窮途末路了？

B： 就我所知，現在日本相當依賴她的一個財政制度審議會。

A： 那是政府機構嗎？它的功用是什麼？

B： 它隸屬日本財政部，是由公司主管、企業人士、學者以及新聞工作人士所組成，它的主要工作是研討日本政府重要事項，包括預算、資遣制度以及會計事宜。

A： 這些專家一起研究如何解決經濟問題？

B： 針對經濟改革，做深度的研究；內容從如何削減開支到調整債務佔國民生產毛額的比例，都是它的研究範圍。

第一步　看中文聽英文；若有疑問，才參考書後的英文。
　　　　（至少 2 次）

第二步　眼看中文，口中隨著 CD，練習中翻英。

第三步　不看中文、耳聽 CD，練習把英文翻成中文；若
　　　　有疑問，才參考書中的中文。

可使用單字

1. 會計年度   fiscal year

2. 生意主管   business executive

3. 財政部   Ministry of Finance

4. 各種福利   settlement

5. 審議   deliberate

6. 立場   standpoint

7. 第三者   a third party

8. 並排   alongside

9. 方法   measure, means, method

10. 方法論   methodology

11. 成型	formulation
12. 提出	submit
13. 和……有關	in regard to
14. 改革	reform
15. 有深度的	in-depth
16. 削減開銷	cut expenditure
17. 使企業合法化	rationalize
18. 具體的	concrete
19. 整合	consolidate
20. 比例	ratio
21. 債務負擔（債務佔國民生產毛額之比例）	debt-to-GDP

22. 以及	as well as
23. 爭論	dispute
24. 蕭條、停滯	stagnation
25. 呆帳	bad bank loan
26. 經濟蕭條	recession
27. 牴觸	conflict
28. 日圓	yen
29. 遣散費	settlement

Petroleum

石油

A： 石油是全世界最重要的商品，石油這樣一路飆漲
已經使世界經濟失去了正常的運作！你知道嗎，
只要一桶漲 15 美元，單單美國就增加 1% 的失業
人口。

B： 真的？爲什麼沒有足夠的石油來降低油價，使它
回穩，以滿足市場的需求？

A： 因爲曾經權傾一時的「石油輸出國家組織」的勢
力逐漸式微，他們對全球油量的持有比例已不如
以往。

B： 怎麼會這樣？

A： 因爲好幾個非石油組織國家也躍入生產！

B： 哪些國家？

A： 俄羅斯、挪威、墨西哥。還有非洲及南美洲都新
發現油田。

B： 既然到處都有石油，價錢爲什麼還居高不下？

A： 因爲只有石油輸出國家組織才會照章行事（＊價錢
方面）。但是，在十個最大的石油供應商中，只有
三個是 OPEC 成員。不過這三位成員就提供全球
一半以上的石油。

B： 既然佔一半以上，他們就可以大聲說話了啊！

A： 那是因爲西方的強國在中東得罪了一大堆石油輸
出國，這次伊拉克戰爭尤其更讓他們憤怒。

B： 可是全部的物品包括交通、材料、房地產、化妝
品……等等的價格都深受影響，而且是立即的！

A： 油價和人類的生活的確息息相關。

第一步　看中文聽英文；若有疑問，才參考書後的英文。
（至少 2 次）

第二步　眼看中文，口中隨著 CD，練習中翻英。

第三步　不看中文、耳聽 CD，練習把英文翻成中文；若
有疑問，才參考書中的中文。

1. 出軌　　　　　　　　derail

2. 採取行動　　　　　　take the action

3. 可負擔的，可忍受的　sustainable

4. 經濟學家　　　　　　economist

5. 關心　　　　　　　　concerned about

6. 一生　　　　　　　　lifetime

7. 桶　　　　　　　　　barrel

8. 石油　　　　　　　　petroleum

9. 快速跳起來　　　　　ramp

Qingming Shang He Tu

(Along the River during the Ching-Ming Festival)

清明上河圖

A： 你在士林故宮博物院有沒有看到一幅「清明上河圖」的卷軸畫？

B： 有啊。那是一幅很長的卷軸，我還買了一把上面

印著這幅畫的絲扇子。看起來很精緻！

A：這幅畫描繪了明朝和清朝的風土民情呢！

B：畫中的河邊有女人洗衣、耍猴戲，還有空中飛人表演。

A：還有孩子玩耍，戲劇表演以及許多好玩的景象。

B：我很喜歡它鮮艷色彩和細膩的筆法。

A：那是西方的畫法，也正反映了清朝畫作的特色。

第一步　看中文聽英文；若有疑問，才參考書後的英文。（至少 2 次）🎧

第二步　眼看中文，口中隨著 CD，練習中翻英。🎧

第三步　不看中文、耳聽 CD，練習把英文翻成中文；若有疑問，才參考書中的中文。🎧

可使用單字

1. 精巧的、偉大的　　　masterful

2. 可打開的畫軸　　　　unfolding

3. 手卷畫軸　　　　　　hand scroll

4. 版片　　　　　　　　version

5. 故宮　　　　　　　　National Palace Museum

6. 統治　　　　　　　　reign

7. 合作　　　　　　　　collaboration

8. 戲劇表演　　　　　　theatrical performance

9. 雜耍空中飛人表演　　acrobatics

10. 雜耍空中飛人　　　　acrobat

11. 國術	martial arts
12. 節慶氣氛	festive air
13. 筆法	brushwork
14. 透視、立體的畫法	perspective
15. 細緻的	exquisite

The Jadeite Cabbage

翠玉白菜

A： 我看看妳的玉鐲。好漂亮哦！

B： 哪裏，妳的墜子才漂亮呢。中國人一直把玉視爲
吉祥之物。

A： 但是玉很難雕刻，費時費力，而且需要有經驗的
人才能雕。

B： 對，主要是依玉石的原狀來刻出最適合的玉器。

以翠玉白菜爲例，這塊玉的顏色有白有綠，有兩隻雕工精緻，栩栩如生的蚱蜢，令人見之心醉。

A：白菜上爲什麼要雕蚱蜢？有什麼意義嗎？

B：蚱蜢在中國古時候，代表了多子多孫。因爲中國以前在古時候是農業社會，需要很多的人手來做農事，所以大家就認爲，多子多孫多福壽。而蚱蜢靜靜待在純淨的、白綠相間的白菜上，代表了純良的家庭必然人丁興旺。

A：眞棒！一件玉器就包含了那麼豐富的文化！

第一步 看中文聽英文；若有疑問，才參考書後的英文。（至少 2 次）

第二步 眼看中文，口中隨著 CD，練習中翻英。

第三步 不看中文、耳聽 CD，練習把英文翻成中文；若有疑問，才參考書中的中文。

1. 製造   manufacture

2. 玉器   jade object

3. 翡翠   jadeite

4. 可觀的   considerable

5. 因此   consequently

6. 主要原則   guiding principle

7. 藝術化的   artistic

8. 源於   derived from

9. 蚱蜢   grasshopper

10. 栩栩如生   lifelikeness

11. 子孫	offspring
12. 多子多孫	fertility
13. 人手	manpower

Patents

專　利

A：我要替我的新發明申請專利。

B：怎麼？你要大量生產嗎？

A：或許吧，所以我才要為我的發明尋求保護啊！

B：對，許多人窮畢生之力研發一項產品，但是往往
　　很快就有許多類似的產品出現，使原先的發明者
　　苦不堪言。

A：和別人的發明比起來，我的發明只是小 case。許多人在研究和實驗方面不知花費了多少時間、金錢、努力，才發明出一樣東西來。

B：所以才有「專利法案」的立法啊！不然，如果研究成果沒有受到保護，還有誰會去投注心力呢！

A：有了「專利法案」，我們就有權利阻止別人來模仿、製造、販售、使用或是進口和這項發明有關的產品或是點子。

B：換句話說，專利權也就是一種獨佔權，但是如果同一個時間有兩個人來申請同一樣東西的專利呢？

A：有關單位所在意的是申請的順序；也就是說，不管誰先發明的，如果有一個以上的人來申請專利，只有第一個申請者才能獲得專利權。

第一步　看中文聽英文；若有疑問，才參考書後的英文。
（至少 2 次）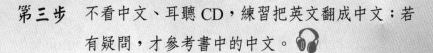

第二步　眼看中文，口中隨著 CD，練習中翻英。

第三步　不看中文、耳聽 CD，練習把英文翻成中文；若
　　　　有疑問，才參考書中的中文。

1. 專利　　　　　patent

2. 提出申請　　　file an application

3. 批准　　　　　grant

4. 獨家　　　　　exclusive

5. 和……相關　　associated with

82

Court Interpretation & Vocabulary

法庭口譯和重要字彙

　　被告被檢察官以殺人未遂起訴。被告辯稱這是一個意外事件，還要控告對方誹謗。

　　但是原告的律師說被告已經有好幾次要殺他的太太，第一次用汽油，但是被害人馬上逃走了；第二次用毒蛇，並沒有成功；第三次則用刀刺，原告忍無可忍，就報警了。

根據檢察官的偵察，這個案子起自多年前被告不僅外遇，還瞞著妻子重婚，結果被原告抓姦，鬧上法庭，結果被判以重婚罪，第三者則被判妨害家庭。

法官聽了被告答辯、再答辯和三度答辯之後，認為被告不但巧辯，歪曲事實，而且手段極其殘忍，當庭判決被告同時犯了縱火、重婚和殺人未遂的併合罪，刑期為終身監禁，並且不得上訴，將案子終結。

第一步 看中文聽英文；若有疑問，才參考書後的英文。（至少 2 次）

第二步 眼看中文，口中隨著 CD，練習中翻英。

第三步 不看中文、耳聽 CD，練習把英文翻成中文；若有疑問，才參考書中的中文。

可使用單字

以下是法庭口譯必備的基本字彙。

1. 最高法院	supreme court
2. 高等法院	high court
3. 地方法院	district court
4. 少年法庭	juvenile court
5. 軍事法庭	martial court
6. 公證	notary
7. 檢察官	prosecutor
8. 檢察長	chief prosecutor
9. 原告	plaintiff, prosecutor

10. 被告	defendant
11. 律師團	bar
12. 法警	court policeman
13. 訴訟、官司	lawsuit
14. 起訴書	indictment
15. 傳票	subpoena (或 citation)
16. 旁聽席	visitor's seats
17. 親自出席	physical presence
18. 代言人	attorney
19. 證人	witness
20. 捏造	fabrication
21. 法律漏洞	legal loophole

22. 自白	confession
23. 誣告	malicious accusation
24. 代罪人	scapegoat
25. 主犯	principal
26. 共犯	accomplice
27. 自衛	self defense
28. 故意……	intentional
29. 惡意……	malicious
30. 證物	evidence
31. 被害人	victim
2. 沒收	confiscate
3. 查封	attach

34. 法外施恩	leniency
35. 和解	settlement (或 compromise)
36. 口供	deposition (或 statement)
37. 翻供證詞	retract testimony
38. 輕罪	misdemeanor
39. 重罪	felony
40. 答辯	defend
41. 二度答辯	rejoinder
42. 三度答辯	rebutter
43. 巧辯	sophistry
44. 歪曲事實	distortion
45. 斥責	reprimand

A Model Court

模範法庭

A： 我不喜歡去法院，那裏的人很不尊重人。

B： 所以我對於洛杉磯的高等法院印象深刻。他們強調對於所有進入法院的人均持「公平、便民、裏外如一，以及熱心、負責」的態度。

A： 「公平」、「熱心」、「負責」意指已非常清楚，但是所講的「便民」和「表裏如一」是什麼意思呢？

B： 根據法院的解釋，所謂的「便民」就是幫助老百姓不但認清自己在法律中所碰到的障礙，而且還要清除這些障礙。而「表裏如一」指的則是不但個人的權利和自由必須被尊重，個人的機密也要受到完全保護，而且法院的工作人員須以具道德和專業的服務態度來對待民眾。

A： 洛杉磯的高等法院真是各地法院要學習的對象！

第一步　看中文聽英文；若有疑問，才參考書後的英文。（至少 2 次）

第二步　眼看中文，口中隨著 CD，練習中翻英。

第三步　不看中文、耳聽 CD，練習把英文翻成中文；若有疑問，才參考書中的中文。

可使用單字

1. 地方法院	local court	
2. 高等法院	superior court	
3. 最高法院	supreme court	
4. 便捷性	accessibility	
5. 操守	dignity	
6. 障礙	barrier	
7. 一致性	integrity	
8. 機密性	confidentiality	
9. 做事	conduct	
0. 合倫理地	ethically	

11. 創新的	innovative
12. 可靠性	accountability

Applying for a US Student Visa

申請赴美留學簽證

A： 我打算明年去美國唸秋季班。我該申請哪一種簽
證呢？

B： 你可以申請 F-1 或是 M-1，但是要符合條件才
行。

A：F-1 是什麼？

B：是發給要念學科的人的學生簽證。F-1 發給你，F-2 則發給你的家人。

A：那 M 又是什麼簽證呀？

B：那是念術科的學生簽證。

A：哦，要具備什麼條件呢？

B：I-20 表格，表示他們已經接受你到一般學校語言班或是職業學校註冊了。

A：到哪裏申請 I-20？

B：學校會寄來，但是這個學校要被 USCIS 承認才行。

A：USCIS 又是什麼？

B：「美國公民和移民服務處」。

A：我需不需要托福之類的成績來證明我的英文程度？

B：不一定，倒是學校會需要。在申請學生簽證時，你可以給他們看你的英文程度證明，也可以給他們看你已經在某所語言學校註冊的證明。

A： 還需要什麼嗎？

B： 你必須證明你有足夠的錢，來就讀整個學程，包括學費、生活費、保險費……等等。

A： 學生簽證難不難申請？

B： 一點也不難。你只要把錢、英文、I-20 準備好就行了。他們是很歡迎優秀的外國學生的！

第一步 看中文聽英文；若有疑問，才參考書後的英文。（至少 2 次）

第二步 眼看中文，口中隨著 CD，練習中翻英。

第三步 不看中文、耳聽 CD，練習把英文翻成中文；若有疑問，才參考書中的中文。

Obtaining a US Work Permit

美國工作許可

A： 我到美國讀書時，可能會想辦法打工。

B： 如果你不是美國公民或永久居民，就得要申請
EAD。

A： EAD 是什麼？

B： 就是 USCIS 所發的工作許可證。沒有這個證明就
不能打工。

A： 這要怎樣申請呢？

B： 去看看他們的網站，而且要記得在原來的 EAD 期
滿之前的六個月就要申請續辦哦！

第一步 看中文聽英文；若有疑問，才參考書後的英文。
（至少 2 次）

第二步 眼看中文，口中隨著 CD，練習中翻英。

第三步 不看中文、耳聽 CD，練習把英文翻成中文；若
有疑問，才參考書中的中文。

1. 永久居民   permanent resident

2. 損壞   mulitate

3. 拼錯了   misspelled

4. 政治庇護   political asylum

5. 暫時的、過渡的   interim

附錄

重要：請勿先看英文，此處僅供聽 CD 有疑問時，做為參考之用。

1. In a Restaurant

A: We are ready to order now.

B: Sure. How can I serve you?

A: I would like to have a medium beefsteak with French fries. And please make them crispy! By the way, no MSG!

B: Sure. What dessert would you like to have? We've got mango pudding, vanilla ice cream and cheesecake!

A: Are they complimentary?

B: Indeed they are! So are the drinks.

A: I am diabetic. Do you carry any unsweetened snacks?

B: We've got unsweetened green tea Jell-O. That's sugar free.

A: That's wonderful. I would like to have unsweetened green tea Jell-O and rose herbal tea, please.

B: Right away!

A: There's no hurry. We are going to hang out around here for at least an hour and a half.

2. In a Clinic

Doc: What is disturbing you? (What's your problem?)

Patient: I keep throwing up, my hands are shaking, I have diarrhea, feel dizzy and nauseated, and I've got a rash all over.

D: Did you eat anything bad? Or are you allergic to anything?

P: I went to a wedding banquet last night. The ketchup that came with the prawns tasted sour.

D: Are any other guests having similar symptoms to yours?

P: Nope! Only me. But I get sick quite often.

D: Your immune system might be weak.

P: What should I do? I almost fainted! I was even staggering on the way here.

D: I will give you an I.V. You must exercise every day for at least 30 minutes, at least 3 times a week. And you must sweat in order to exercise your internal organs and detoxify your body!

3. Making Dumplings

Mother:　I suddenly feel like having some pot stickers and dumplings. Shall we make some today?

Daughter:　Sure! We can buy some dough at the supermarket, and then we'll prepare the filling.

M:　What dumpling would you like to eat? Leeks with pork or cabbage with beef? Or yummy, crispy pot stickers?

D:　Why don't we have all three of them?

M:　That would be too troublesome. And I just remembered that pot stickers are a bit too greasy. I'd better take something light since I have hypertension now.

D:　In that case, we'll have lean pork with leeks, plus bean noodles, ginger, and baby shrimps.

M:　Good. And the sauce will be garlic, basil, green onion, sesame oil, vinegar and soybean sauce.

D:　And chili sauce! But not too much soybean sauce. It has preservatives!

M:　Would you also like to have hot and sour soup or corn porridge?

D:　Mom, my mouth is watering!

4. Taking Care of Each Other

Husband: My throat itches.

Wife: There are pears in the frig. I'll go buy some loquats. I've been told that loquats and pears cease coughing.

H: That's really sweet of you. You are a great wife.

W: Thanks. But you also took care of me last time when I had constipation.

H: That was my job. We are both getting old, and need to take care of each other. Not to mention that you have migraines, and I've got high-cholesterol. We are all that we've got for each other!

W: I cannot agree more. And I really appreciate your lifelong loyalty to me.

H: Thanks. I am so grateful to your companionship through all the ups and downs in our lives.

5. Parents Went Out

A: Mom and dad are out. Why don't we reorganize everything?

B: How?

A: You put the rattan chair by the screen; I'll push the piano between the rocking chair and the buffet.

B: But the piano is so heavy. I'll help you.

A: No need. It's got castors.

B: Then I'll give the kitchen a general clean up. I'll do the sink, cupboard, chopping board, rice cooker and lid.

A: Cool. Then I'll do the dresser, the toilet and the mirror.

B: Aren't our parents lucky to have daughters like us?

A: What about last time when you talked back to mom and almost gave her apoplexy?

B: You just had to say it, right?

6. Volcanic Eruptions

Tourist: Why is that mountain smoking?

Tour guide: That's an active volcano.   It has been smoking ever since it erupted 20 years ago.

Tourist: I thought it was dormant.   Is it dangerous?   What if it erupts again?

Tour guide: Do not worry. We are leaving soon after lunch.

Tourist: Last time I saw on the *Discovery* Channel, lava rolled down all the way to the foot of the mountain during an eruption. It was horrible!

Tour guide: That's right.   You know quite a few volcano experts walk close to the craters for studying?

Tourist: Yeah! I heard on TV that two volcano experts got burned to death during a volcanic eruption.

7. Seeing a Fortune-Teller

Fortune-teller: Your eyes are clear and shining, and your nose is fleshy. You must be rich and smart.

Customer: But I don't even have my own apartment yet. I can't even afford the down payment.

F: There's no hurry. You've got large ear lobes and a long philtrum. You will live long and well.

C: Is that so? That is great! How long will I live? When will I get rich?

F: As a fortune-teller, I cannot reveal the secret of your life. When it's time, it's time! But your teeth are a bit messy; you'd better have them fixed.

C: But braces are expensive. They could cost at least US$2,500 and I am already 25, isn't it too late?

F: Better late than never.

C: What about yourself? Did you ever read your own life?

F: I did, a long time ago! You know what? I was meant to be a fortune-teller.

8. Doing Mathematics

A: Oh, No! It's math again! I hate math!

B: Why? I think the kingdom of math is fantastic! Especially when you are able to solve a problem. That kind of excitement is beyond description!

A: Those triangles, squares, rectangles, rhombuses, trapeziums, areas and circumferences give me headaches.

B: That's geometry! But even geometry can be fun! It's challenging to figure out the areas, masses, and etc. from different shapes and figures!

A: Numbers are annoying too! Odds, evens, squares, powers, square roots, etc.

B: You don't have to worry. You are not a science or engineering major. All you need to do is addition, subtraction, multiplication, and division either mentally or with a calculator.

A: Especially applications, right?

B: There you go! That's all math means to you!

9. Going to a Concert

A: Hey. I've got two concert tickets. Do you wanna go?

B: Whose concert? It's not the three tenors, is it?

A: In your dreams.　But this isn't bad, either --- It's the concert of Celine Dion. And she's going to have a great band to accompany her.　That conductor is one of the best in the world.

B: Really? I can hardly wait.

A: The TV says that she made around US$970,000,000 last year.

B: Oh, my goodness. I am making only US$300/month. It's not fair!

A: You mustn't think so. A good health and a grateful heart are the most valuable things in the world! Just think of it this way: You wouldn't want to fret about being kidnapped, and you wouldn't want to be stared at when you have smelly tofu on the roadside, would you?

B: You've got a point there! Besides, I don't have their voices!

A: That's the point! We can have some beef noodles before going to the concert. C'est la vie!

10. Math Applications (1) — Living Expenses

A: David makes US$900 per month and pays US$200 for his car loan, US$50 for gas and $100 for the apartment rent, US$20 on health insurance. Everyday he spends $15 on food, and oh, I almost forgot, around US$30 on entertainment. Good thing that he has a month and a half bonus at the end of year. So my question is how much money can he save per year?

B: Hold on. I will get my calculator.

1. US$900 x 13.5 = US$12,150, this is his yearly income. Let me jot it down so I won't forget.
2. Ok. Then US$15 on food, times 365 days, equals US$5,475 a year.
3. And US$200 on car plus US$50 on gas, plus again US$100 rent, $20 on health insurance, $30 on entertainment, that's US$400; then times 12 months, and it comes to US$4800 for the whole year expenses. Oops, I missed the $5,475 on food. So it should be $10,275 altogether.
4. So the total income $12,150 minus the total expenses $10,275 he should be able to save $1,875 per year.

A: What if he wishes to buy an apartment? For example, if the apartment costs US$200,000, can he afford it?

B: Let's see. $200,000 ÷ 1,875 = 106.66…. Wow! That's impossible! It'll take more than 106 years!

A: That's what mortgages are for! Let's calculate the interest.

B: Never mind. Next time! My head is stuffed!

11. Math Applications (II) — Savings and Mortgages

A: Let's do an easy math problem.

B: Ok. I'll get a pen, paper and a calculator.

A: Suppose there is US$200,000 mortgage with 5% yearly interest rate, how much is the interest?

B: Let's see. 200,000 x 0.05 = 10,000.

A: I meant the interest per month.

B: Right. Divided by 12 = 833.333.

A: You got it right! Let's now do another math on saving. If you have $100,000 in the bank with a yearly interest rate of 2%. How much can you have in a year for your principal and gains?

B: 100,000 x 1.02 = 102,000

A: You got it right again.

12. Self-Introduction

I come from the countryside. My father, a farmer, and my mother, a typical housewife, are busy from morning till night.

My 23-year-old sister is upset because she has been jobless since graduation last year. My 17-year-old brother, an eleventh grader, does great in school and intends to go to law school after graduating from high school. He hopes that he will be able to earn respect and make a fortune while advocating justice for the needy. I think that he's being a bit naïve, because I've heard that many lawyers today are living hand to mouth.

As for myself, I've always been fascinated with art and literature. I became fond of painting and writing in junior high school, one of the reasons why I am in the English department. My English is so poor that I know I must do something about it.

Success cannot be achieved without effort, luck and prudence. I spare no effort, and was lucky enough to have met a remarkable English teacher who taught us the right way to learn excellent English, making us improve every single day, and taught us to lead our lives with prudence and cheerfulness, including self-discipline, a good health, a beautiful heart, and lots of smiles!

13. The Cost of Living (Number Training)

Over time, the cost-of-living index rose along with inflation. Prices of objects from small as a pencil to large as a house have been hiked up by time. For example, college tuition costing US$1,000-2,000 per semester was only a few hundred dollars in the 1980s. Added with living expenses, utilities, miscellaneous, allowances, and rent, at least US$5,000 slipped from my parents' pockets per semester. Altogether, my 4 years in college will cost me about US$40,000! My father, a government employee, and my mother, who has not been employed ever since she got laid off a few years ago, live hand-to-mouth. Good thing that I am the only child. Imagine how miserable it would be if they had two or three more kids!

14. Accurate Pronunciation

Sometime within the past 10 years a new trend has appeared in the field of English teaching that emphasizes the goal that non-English speakers learning English become effective at communication. This trend implies that "communication" is all that matters and that other elements, such as pronunciation, intonation and even grammar, aren't important. Of course rhetoric, or the beauty of the language, isn't concerned important, either.

Indeed, it is never easy for anyone to learn any foreign language, let alone to speak and write it accurately or even "beautifully." Nonetheless, I am strongly convinced that our young and dynamic students with their great memories, who will soon step into extremely competitive fields, deserve to be taught the best. English majors should be assured of learning to speak and write excellent English in order to be ready for the job market of the future and, if they are to join the teaching field, to bring even further contributions to society.

Once a high-ranking employee of an American radio station in China, who loves Chinese culture, expressed his idea of teaching Chinese students, "I do not really demand too much from my students. I think the pronunciation, intonation, grammar and whatsoever do not need to be emphasized because it'll be good enough for them to communicate effectively in English. After all, English IS a foreign language to them." I immediately asked, "Would your station hire someone who has a very strong command of English, but speaks with some Chinese accent?" He replied without hesitation, "We tried once, but people wrote in to complain!" I felt very sorry for our students because people have given up on them even before they have graduated.

15. Native Intonation

Very beautiful English requires beautiful "intonation" in addition to accurate pronunciation. Chinese is ruled by five tones that are not found in English. As a result, Chinese students read English at their own will, showing very plain and messy intonation. This is an extremely common mistake among English majors in local universities.

Students will find that it pays off to pay more attention to the tone of English because a beautiful tone in English can sound like a little running creek that flows smoothly and beautifully. On the contrary, a very plain tone can make a student sound like a monk chanting. The English tone is meant to be alive; it goes up and down with the speaker's emotions. Fortunately for students, certain basic rules can be applied to the tone, which makes it easier to learn what seems to gallop freely and widely in the kingdom of enunciation.

The pitch of English is very important for Chinese students to learn because native English speakers understand different emotions in the same words and sentences through the use of different tones.

16. Posture

Posture on stage is indispensable for interpreters.

Many Chinesee students who express themselves vibrantly, confidently and even shrewdly in Chinese become totally different once they step on stage to speak in English. Rigidity replaces their animation, timidity their confidence, and hesitation replaces shrewdness -- and all these changes have psychological roots! It can't just be guilt at not mastering a foreign language. I see many Americans who do not speak Chinese and many Europeans who do not speak English, yet I have never seen any of them feeling inferior to others just because they do not speak a foreign language fluently.

Ever since the Ching dynasty, when China was defeated by Western opium and cannons, Chinese people have been sculpted by the country and society to feel inferior to Westerners. Such a misconception has misled many of our students to feel ineffectual if they cannot speak English in front of Westerners. It is such a psychological difficulty for them that it makes them feel as though giving English speeches in front of people is a torture. This isn't right!

Whatever and however we speak and look and feel should not be affected by the nationality or social status of the listener. To sum up, a competent interpreter should at least pay attention to the following posture:

1. First Impression
2. Voice Production
3. Posture and Gestures
4. Clothing
5. Empathy
6. Leaving the stage properly

17. Delivering an Impromptu English Speech (I)

Very often, while attending English speech contests, you will need to present an impromptu speech for the final, and five to 10 minutes are usually allowed for preparation. Let's see how to prepare an impressive script in just three minutes.

First of all, very strong ability in English is the most fundamental element for impromptu speeches. A Chinese saying, "One minute's performance on the stage requires 10 years' work" describes perfectly the situation of an English impromptu speech presented by Chinese. It is for this reason that the following should be done before you proceed with preparing any impromptu speech:

1. Have you already accumulated a wide range of vocabulary?
2. Have you been well trained to speak English at the speed that is used by native English speakers?
3. Have you already learned a very charming posture to display on stage?
4. Have you already learned accurate pronunciation and intonation?
5. Have you already learned excellent voice production, including the vocal clarity, texture, volume and emotions?

18. Delivering an Impromptu English Speech (II)

Unfortunately, even the above-mentioned elements – impressive as they are -- aren't all you need for preparing impromptu speeches. The following can immediately and effectively help. Once the topic is given, you may very rapidly work as follows:

1. Assure your stance: What stance are you taking for the topic? Be very specific. No ambiguity, no empty talk! (Time for preparation: 5-10 seconds)

2. Explain your stance: Give any convincing reasons to explain why you chose that stance. (20 seconds)

3. Give examples: Find very active examples to support your stance. Search from your memory, understanding, observation, knowledge or even imagination. Two-three examples are required for a three-minute speech. (30 seconds)

4. Collect vocabulary: You may bring *Simultaneous Interpretation* with you and find 10-15 very impressive words. Of course, these words should already be familiar to you in order to maintain proficiency. (1 minute)

5. Find wise sayings: Find two to three very wise sayings from "Simultaneous Interpretation" or any nice book. Again, those sayings should already be familiar to you. (20 seconds)

6. Rapidly outline: Write down on paper your key words for the introduction, body and conclusion. (1-1.5 minutes)

19. Christianity

A: I think all the religions are aiming for the same thing: altruism!

B: Not exactly. Christianity seeks true freedom, which is not earned through good works.

A: What do you mean by true freedom?

B: Humans are limited in terms of love, forgiveness and mercy. But Jesus' love and power make people brand new --- they become full of joy, love, faith and finally, free from anger, greed, and lying, which is true freedom.

A: What's the difference between Christianity and Catholicism?

B: They are practically the same. To my knowledge, Christianity pays less attention to rituals and is not primarily churchgoing or ceremonies.

A: What is Christianity then?

B: It's Christ in you. For example, humans choose whom to love, but Jesus Christ, the flesh of god, was crucified for sinners for making himself atonement for washing away their sins.

A: I don't get it.

B: As people don't sacrifice with handicapped animals or withered fruits to please god and ask to be forgiven, Jesus Christ who had never sinned used himself as an impeccable sacrifice for us.

A: Most Christians are very loving, but some are very lousy.

B: Christians enjoy sharing Christ's endless love and joy with others. As for those who aren't as good, are condemned by Jesus as hypocrites.

20. Buddhism (I)

A: A majority of Taiwanese residents are Buddhists. What do they believe?

B: Buddhism basically explores human suffering and mercy.

A: They worship gods and goddesses?

B: As a matter of fact, they follow the doctrines by Sakyamuni who concluded that humans suffer from birth, aging, sickness, death, failure, and the impermanence of pleasure.

A: So does Buddhism provide any way out?

B: Pretty hard, because all the suffering stems from greed, hatred and delusion, which are congenital. .

A: Ya, I understand. For example, the desire for fame and wealth, the eager to possess and to control, all lead to fear, anger, jealousy, disappointment, and even anxiety.

B: That's unfortunately so true and miserable.

21. Buddhism (II)

A: How can suffering cease in Christianity and Buddhism?

B: Christians are baptized in Christ and thus peace replaces anxiety, love replaces selfishness, forgiveness anger, and hope fear.

A: Whereas Buddhists achieve those through good deeds?

B: Yes, Buddhists believe that suffering won't cease until Nirvana, and their fundamental hope is reincarnation.

A: I know. Reincarnation is the concept about cycling; but what's Nirvana?

B: After many cycles of birth, aging, sickness and death, humans finally attain Nirvana (when they die) if they can finally release their attachment to desire. This is the final liberation from suffering.

A: And reincarnation is a matter of rebirth?

B: Yes, and it involves karma.

A: What karma?

B: A human is reborn as a human even a god if good karma ripens.

A: What if bad karma ripens?

B: Then he/she is reborn into a lower state, such as a pig, a hungry ghost, or even is permanently imprisoned in Hades if negative karma ripens.

A: That explains why Buddhists chant the sutras, burn incense-sticks, conduct good deeds --- all for the purpose of accumulating secret merits!

B: You cannot deny that many Buddhists are very lenient, but many of them also are doing these for the reincarnation.

22. Losing Weight

A: Gosh, how I wish to lose 5 kilos in a week.

B: But the healthiest way to lose weight is not necessarily the quickest!

A: I've been jogging for one hour a day consecutively for a whole week!

B: I wouldn't recommend trendy weight loss plans, crash diets or drastic increases in exercise.

A: Why not? Isn't exercise combined with a healthy diet highly recommended by doctors?

B: But changes must be gradual.

A: I see.

B: You know exercise itself has anti-cancer benefits?

A: I do. According to a medical report, staying physically active and eating right can cut cancer risk by a large percentage!

B: What about hypnotherapy? Does it help with weight management as well?

A: That's beyond my knowledge.

23. A Joyful Heart Is the Best Medicine

I once read an article by a prestigious pathologist, Dr. Li Feng of Taiwan University Hospital, in which she mentioned her successful experience in fighting cancer. Every morning after she gets up, she immediately drinks a large glass of good water to clean her intestines, and then meditates for 5 minutes, and she eats her grain, cereal, and fruit. This is what she calls a "detoxifying breakfast."

Dr. Li Feng exercises everyday and laughs a lot! She said, "Under the microscope our cells look full and shining when we are happy, but they look wrinkled when we are stressed."

The Bible says well, "A joyful heart is the best medicine while a sad spirit crashes the bones." Dr. Dale Carnegie also said that according to statistics, approximately 99% of what we are afraid that might happen actually won't happen. Indeed after 10 years when we look back, those things that almost killed us then do not matter any more. I would say true wisdom is found in great happiness!

24. Teeth Whitening

A: My teeth are a bit yellowish. I need to have them bleached.

B: White teeth indeed look pleasant. Are you going to use the in-office method or the home method?

A: What's the "in-office" method?

B: It puts a strong bleaching agent over your isolated teeth first, and then uses a special light to assist the bleaching. This method is better for those who have stains or streaks on teeth. One hour should be enough for the whole process.

A: And the "home" method?

B: It makes trays to fit into your mouth and fills them with bleaching materials. You wear them for a few minutes to a few hours a day, and noticeable results can be expected in just a few days. It's less costly.

A: How long can the results last?

B: Results vary from individual to individual. But an unfortunate fact is that the bleached teeth usually become yellowish again in a few months.

25. Why Has My Voice Turned Hoarse?

A: My voice has been hoarse for more than a year.

B: What happened?

A: Early last year I got bronchitis, but I went on teaching and giving speeches still.

B: So your vocal cords weren't properly rested.

A: What are the major factors which cause hoarseness anyway?

B: It could be related to the problem either in your vocal cords or in the nerves, which supply the vocal cords.

A: My voice sounds slightly raspy and breathy.

B: Do you have difficulty breathing?

A: Not at all.

B: Is there a lump in your neck or around your ears? A lump may be a sign of cancer if it has grown slowly and feels hard; it may be just infection if it has grown quickly and is very tender.

A: Nope! No lump!

B: Hoarseness is also associated with smoking and alcoholism, but I know you don't smoke or drink.

A: I don't.

B: Did you see an ENT doctor (specialist)?

A: Two of them! They both told me to remain absolutely "mute" for 10 days, which was impossible for me.

B: There you go!

26. Eyestrain, Astigmatism and Myopia

A: My eyes itch.　I also suffer from burning, chronic redness, and grittiness in my eyes.

B: This is some form of dry eye syndrome.

A: Dry eye?　What should I do?

B: Your ophthalmologist can prescribe treatment to help alleviate the symptoms.

A: By the way, my vision is blurred, but I'm not near-sighted.

B: Then you probably have astigmatism.

A: What is astigmatism anyway?

B: It is a refractive error in which light rays entering the eye don't focus on a single point.

A: And that causes a distortion or blurring of images?

B: Exactly.　Where these images focus depends on whether the astigmatism is associated with myopia or hyperopia.

A: So how should I take care of my eyes?

B: Take little breaks every 15 minutes to rest your eyes when you watch TV or use the computer in order not to get eyestrain.

27. Immune from Depression

A: Why are we seeing more people suffering from depression than before?

B: Because the economy recession, high unemployment rate, challenging interpersonal relationships and vulnerable human nature are all making us anxious.

A: What can we do for self-rescue?

B: Life is too short to resent for the past or fret about the future. Appreciate and focus on the etát-être.

A: I can't stop splitting hairs when I'm under pressure.

B: Exercise then! Exercise boosts a natural chemical called endorphin in your body that makes you feel good and depression free.

A: But I can't reach my goals, which is making me nervous!

B: Set reachable goals and celebrate each small success.

A: I enjoy my solitude. But is it necessary to socialize?

B: Make an effort to see a comedian movie or go to a restaurant with a friend. Share your feelings with others, and laugh a lot!

28. Welcome to the Party!

A: My son is getting married next month. I'm tangled with a multitude of feelings! Am I losing him?

B: "Losing" is an incorrect word because he is not your property, and he'll have to blaze his own trail.

A: But he is my flesh and bones!

B: *The Bible* says, "A man will leave his parents and be united to his wife." You are no more entitled to know everything about him.

A: That's sad. Can't I even know whom they entertain or how much money they make?

B: Worse. Don't even complain if their visits are too infrequent. And don't ask to be included for their family plans --- they'll invite you if they want you to join them.

A: What if my daughter-in-law misbehaves?

B: That's not your concern. What if YOUR son misbehaves? Be a peacemaker --- never sow discords between them, and don't make yourself an eyesore!

A: But I'll feel so alone without him around.

B: Filial piety is a beautiful virtue and is richly blessed, but it has to be voluntary. Why don't you develop your own friendship and hobbies? It'll be more rewarding to be with friends.

A: Should I please my daughter-in-law from time to time?

B: That'll be a taxing and thankless job. But do generously compliment her and say thank you when thanks are due.

A: So I'll just live my own life and keep my nose clean and clear? But that's miserable!

B: Welcome to the Party! Just think on the bright side: you may have the sweetest kids on earth!

29.　Smoking Jeopardizes Health

A:　A friend of mine died of cancer at only 42 years old.　He was a smoker all right, in addition to another sad fact that he was often exposed in secondhand cigarette smoke.

B:　Right.　Researches have indicated that in the States lung cancer is not reserved for men only, and about 90% of all lung cancer deaths among women are from smoking!

A:　And I've heard that lung cancer even kills more women than breast cancer.

B:　What's cancer anyway? All I know is it's malignant cells!

A:　When certain body cells don't function right and divide rapidly, they produce too much tissue, which gradually forms a tumor.

B:　It's known that the best way to prevent lung cancer is to quit smoking.

A:　Right.　The sooner a person quits the better for everyone!　Are you also aware that smoking interferes with post-surgery healing?

B:　I've never heard of that.

A:　Smoking may constrict blood vessels and thus decrease blood flow all over the body.　And if someone has general anesthesia and smokes during the post-operative healing period, he may cough very hard, leading to internal bleeding!

30. Oral Hygiene

A: My molar hurts; I probably have a tooth cavity.

B: When was last time you saw a dentist?

A: Two years ago.

B: You need a scaling every six months. Like a machine, our body gets problems emerging along with the increase of age.

A: Tell me about it! I have noticed all the effects of aging on me: graying hair, wrinkles, spots, and a variety of aches and pains which weren't there before.

B: The mouth is also hit by advancing age. You know bacteria get on your teeth, gums, lips, tongue, and even throat?

A: How can I remove them?

B: Some bacteria aren't harmful, and some are even helpful. Only certain types of them attaching themselves to the enamel need to be removed, or they'll multiply in no time.

A: And they become plaque?

B: Close. The proteins in your saliva mix in the bacteria and form a whitish film on the teeth. The film is called "plaque" and causes cavities!

31. Very Annoying Tinnitus

A: I am hearing noise in my ears! It's so annoying!

B: Did you see an ENT doctor?

A: I did. He said I lack vitamin B12. What does vitamin B12 have to do with tinnitus?

B: Because tinnitus has something to do with nerves, and vitamin B12 plays a critical role whenever it comes to nerves!

A: I don't get it.

B: A vitamin B12 deficiency may raise our blood levels of a specific amino acid which is toxic to nerves.

A: How much percent of tinnitus victims suffer from vitamin B12 deficiency?

B: I don't know the exact percentage, but it can be anywhere between 10 and 20. You should also know that long-term exposure to noise might deplete your body levels of B12, too!

A: So it's a vicious circle!

B: Right. To protect your ears, get enough B12 intakes, don't pick them with Q-tips, don't wear Walkman, and always keep music down!

32. Cancer-Blocking

A: I'm seeing cancers taking many lives away! What's going on?

B: Do you know that just making a few moderate changes in our lives can prevent most cancers?

A: I know.   As long as 30 years ago, an American Institute, saying that nearly 70% of all cancers were associated with our habits, released this landmark research report.   Now the percentage is higher!

B: Air pollution, water contamination, fertilizers, antibiotics and hormones used on livestock, etc. are all putting toxins into our body.

A: That makes exercise indispensable because malignant cells can't grow in sufficient oxygen.

B: Adopting a healthy diet also reduces cancer risk.   Do you know what cancer-protective fruits and vegetables are?

A: Cruciferous vegetables, such as broccoli, cauliflower, turnips, etc. are some of them.

B: Also all the dark green vegetables, dried nuts, sweet potatoes, ginger, garlic, cacti, blue berries, kiwis, dragon fruits, onions and tomatoes.

33. I Loathe Cotics!

A: Would you like to try some MDMA?

B: Over my dead body!

A: I would like to try for kicks.　I've heard it'll give us great muscular coordination and pleasurable feeling.　You can imagine how remarkable it is by its street names: Ecstasy and Hug!

B: I know way better than that.　It's also called Love and XTC.

A: No kidding!　I thought you were geeky!

B: I'm not a geek, ok?　I'm just wise enough not to be an unfortunate.

A: Come on, how bad can it be?　It can reduce your stress and make you high; besides, small doses won't hook you up.

B: That's what drug addicts always say in the first place.　They are just trying to drag you in by hook or by crook.　No, thanks!　You may keep this brainwashing for yourself.

A: But it'll be very soothing!

B: Research indicates that MDMA is neurotoxic.　It affects your mood, aggression, sleep, etc. because its primary effects are in the brain.　And I don't want to lose my memory in my teens!

A: Does it cause any physical damages as well?

B: Absolutely.   It causes liver, kidney and cardiovascular system failure.

A: That's horrible!   What should I do then when I feel depressed, nervous or anxious?

B: Learn some stress-management techniques.   Never split hairs!

A: And have a healthy diet and exercise a lot for detoxifying the body?

B: There you go!

34. Acquiring Immunity

Two very good books that I recently read, "無毒一身輕" (meaning "detoxifying your body") by Dr. Lin Guang-chang and "來自身體的聲音" by a Greek doctor, Dimitrios Lennis, both teach us how to help ourselves. I think their knowledge of the immune system should be highly esteemed.

First of all, not all the so-called "colds" need to be medically treated. Our body has miraculous healing power as long as we have strong natural defense mechanisms. In other words, we need to bring the best out of our immune system.

These two books mention a prevailing concept of maintaining good health. The three elements that decide our health are food, body, and mind. Our immune functions all rely on these three factors.

35. The First Defense of Immune System

According to Dr. Lennis, our immune system's first line of defense is our skin, including the skin that we see and the mucous in our nose, mouth, and the internal digestive organs, such as the mucus from nose and saliva. Our skin protects us from being attacked, even though we often harm it.   For example, we don't drink enough water, making the throat dry and thus not having enough mucus and saliva to block viruses; or we eat too cold, too hot, or too spicy food, or talk too much or too loud; or we drink wine and takes in MSG, and thus damage the throat; or we stay too long in an air-conditioned room, making our mouth and nose dry, etc... all these weaken the first line of defense of our immune system.

As a result, please drink plenty of fluids, take good care of our skin, including our nose and mouth, etc. to well establish our first line of defense.

36. Inflammation Makes the Body a War Zone

You might have never imagined that to maintain a good health, the second line of defense is not to get inflamed.

Dr. Lennis mentions in his book that inflammation, a warfare in our body, making our body a war-ridden battlefield. Our immune system would rise immediately to fight against any inflammation in our body, meanwhile and unfortunately, it also harms our healthy cells. Lupus Erythematosus (L.E.), psoriasis, thyroid diseases, even cancer, etc. all belong to such a category.

Dr. Lennis thus emphasized that we'll surrender to diseases if we do not properly manage inflammations.

37.   The Consequences of Inflammation

In addition, Dr. Lin and Dr. Lennis warned that what we eat and use causes inflammations of various levels in us, including preservatives, insecticides, artificial pigments, artificial flavors, free radicals, contaminated air and water and food which cause allergies, such as eggs, meat, including seafood, etc.   Therefore, we must be careful about what we eat and drink to minimize the toxins in the body.

The books also mention that fatigue, dizziness, stuffy nose, rash, itchiness, coughing, dermatitis, eczema, even psychological and mental discomforts, including depression, obesity, high-cholesterol, unstable levels of blood sugar, diabetes, unequal secretion of hormones, cardiovascular diseases, stroke, backaches, arthritis, etc. during the primitive stage of inflammation.

Dr. Lin and Dr. Lennis alert that in addition to the above-mentioned ones, new problems may appear, such as gastric ulcer, cancer, female problems, even bad teeth, Alzheimer's disease and many other symptoms related to aging when the immune system is severely jeopardized.

Gosh, to protect our first and second lines of defense, we do need to drink lots and lots of fluids, take lots of rest, watch our diet, stay away from where viruses or germs may gather, and most of all, rejoice all the time!

38. Zygote →Embryo → Fetus

Testicles produce sperm when they mature whereas ovaries already have from 30,000- 40,000 ovums when the female baby is born. This also explains why senior mothers-to-be need to be extra prudent because their ovums are becoming less healthy after having been exposed to radioactive materials such as x-rays, air and chemical pollutions, injuries, aging, etc.

An ovum and a sperm are fertilized into a zygote in which our DNAs, or what we know of as "genes" which decide our characteristics, exist. The chromosomes inside the DNA not only decide the gender, but also decide the complexion, height, the looks on the face, hair color, hair texture (including whether it is straight or curly), and even the personality and diseases in the future.

It has been medically proven that hereditary diseases include diabetes, hemophilia, mental diseases, Mongolian idiocy, allergies, and even cancer and all different kinds of cardiovascular diseases.   Fortunately, the technological amniocentesis which is done usually 15 to 18 weeks after a woman's last menstrual period and CVS (chorionic villus sampling, which is usually done between 10 and 12 weeks) help us know in advance whether the baby is going to have chromosomal and genetic birth defects.   Just for your reference, we Orientals usually adopt these two technologies for knowing the gender of the baby-to-be.

39. Do Not Surrender to Your Fate!

Still, we cannot just succumb our health to our genes, allowing them to decide our whole life.   We Chinese believe that several factors lead to one's fate: Destiny, luck, feng-shui, good deeds, and knowledge. Thus I would rather choose to believe that our heads decide our fates.   For example, children of diabetic parents can be taught careful diet control from childhood (such as to stay away from sweetened stuff), and to get into the habit of doing regular exercise and taking sufficient rests. Another example comes to those whose parent/parents have mental problems should be taught to think positively and joyfully, never overly calculative, having both high EQ and AQ, etc.

As what the pathologist, Dr. Li Feng of Taiwan University Hospital said, our cells appear full and juicy while we are happy and they become dry and withered when we are stressed --- We really cannot afford to frown. Give me a smile.

40. I.V. (Intravenous)

A friend of mine was hit by a car day before yesterday. He has a full cast o his right leg that went from his foot up to his thigh, then around his waist with an opening for his lower abdomen, genital area and butt. He also sustained internal injuries --- his pancreas, a vital organ in his abdomen, was hurt form the impact of the car. The pancreas is responsible for secreting into the intestines certain enzymes that are important for digesting food. Another function of the pancreas is to manufacture insulin, which helps food that is turned into blood sugar get from the blood into tissues throughout the body.

While his pancreas is healing, he is not allowed to eat any food by mouth. In order for him to still get the fluid, nutrients and vitamins that his body requires, An I.V. is attached to him by inserting a needle into a vein in his hand. I.V. is the medical abbreviation for the word intravenous, meaning "within the vein." Though my friend can walk around with this, he has to be very careful not to pull it out accidentally. The doctors and nurses regularly check the area where the I.V. is attached to guard against infection.

41. Cosmetic Surgeries (Plastic Surgeries)

Seeing an increasing number of those who actually went for cosmetic surgeries, we might as well embrace this very interesting topic. Supported by strong science and extensive technical training, plastic surgeons now offer both men and women choices in the aesthetic treatment field, particularly related to facial makeover.

Procedures such as face-lift, brow lift, eyelid surgery, neck lift surgery, eliminating laughing lines, etc. now provide dramatic improvements countering the forces of aging.

As a result, men and women take cosmetic surgeries in the hope hat they can gain the upper hand on the aging process because their refreshed appearance may literally "roll back time".

42. Rhinoplasty (Nose Plastic Surgery) & Breast Augmentation

1) The Nose Job

It's amazing that the noses of most girls in Taipei and Shanghai have suddenly grown tall, which truly adds beauty to the view of these two cities. As a matter of fact, according to cosmetic surgeons, nose reshaping cosmetic surgery, or the "nose job", as we know of, is the most popular procedures undertaken in the market. Although numerous cosmetic surgery candidates experience a repeat treatment, a significant number of first-time surgery candidates do not hesitate to enter the marketplace.

2) Breast Augmentation

Can you believe that quite a few college girls are saving money for breast augmentation surgeries?

One area on us that's greatly impacted by body physiology and the aging process is our breasts because time, aging, gravity, including childbirth and breast feeding (which is actually the best for the mother and the baby), generally produce a tendency towards sagging. But you may need to reconsider if you are planning a breast augmentation surgery for pleasing your boyfriend/husband. After all, beauty is in the eye of the beholder.

43. Botox Injections

TV often propagandizes the amazing effects of Botox. But do Botox injections produce any dangerous side effects? They actually do. Most patients experience limited side effects even though they are given proper dosages and a hygienic environment, localized tenderness, some bruising, swelling and sensitivity, etc. may last a week. In addition, muscular weakness is a common sensation, which is a natural outcome of Botox as the toxin spreads within the muscle tissue areas. Very few people may even experience problems in talking, swallowing or breathing, and that's when you need to see a doctor immediately!

44. Anesthesia

People often ignore the fact that anesthesia is an integral part of your surgical experience.   You need to have some basic knowledge about anesthesia in order not to invite feelings of helplessness and anxiety.

What do you ought to know?   Some people may have a slight feeling of nausea during the immediate postoperative period, which will pass quickly.   Some patients may feel slightly lethargic for the first few hours after surgery --- but this will wear off.

These possible consequences depend on how much you individually react to the anesthesia. Some people may have after effects even with slight amounts of sedation. It is thus mandatory that you be observed during the immediate post-operative period. A trained nursing staff must be available.

45. The Skills of Negotiating

A: Could you teach me the skills of negotiating?

B: I'll try.   You first need to identify your exact expectation.   Don't waffle.

A: Then what?

B: Also try to identify the interests of the other party — both personally and professionally — so you can construct an appealing offer if necessary.

A: How do I locate their crucial interests?

B: A skilled negotiator asks lots of questions.   By doing this you gain information on the other party's position while demonstrating your passion for mutually beneficial results.

A: And do I gain the upper hand by striking first?

B: Not at all.   It's gracious to let the other party open the negotiation session.

A: What if the atmosphere is getting unpleasant?   And what do I do if I hear sarcastic remarks?

B: Don't take it personally.   Stay issue-oriented even if you sense hostility.

A: What if I lose ground?

B: Taking a break makes you feel refreshed and recharged.   But remember to review the agreements so far when you return.

A: What if we can't reach any consensus?

B: No big deal.　The real spirit of negotiating is to create a win-win situation.　Just set the date and time for another meeting.　But you should be fully prepared for a very brainstorming session!

46. The Skills of Debating

A: Remember last time I mentioned the real spirit of negotiation?

B: Yes. It's to create a win-win situation. Could you also teach me some tips for debating?

A: Let's see. There's no specific way to debate. You can be calm and restrained; but you can also be loud and funny.

B: I prefer to be calm and restrained.

A: But you need to talk fast enough to sound shrewd and resourceful, especially when you're attending an English debate. A fast pace also allows you time to fully express yourself.

B: And my attitude during the whole process of debating? Is it blow-for-blow?

A: Aggressively attack, but very calmly advance your own arguments. Never talk glibly!

B: What should I wear for a debate contest?

A: It may aid the subconscious assessment of teamwork if the whole team are attired to the same level of formality.

B: How do I start the debate if I'm on the pro side?

A: Define the motion and justify it.

B: What if I am on the con side?

A: Respond to the definition, stating why it isn't proper.

B: How do I end the debate?

A: A logically challenging ending always sounds powerful and persuasive!

B: Is there anything else I should know?

A: Just keep in mind that a good and humorous debater is always more impressive than simply a good one.

47. Don't Freak out, Moms and Dads!

A: Hey, get a hold of yourself! What are you fuming over this time?

B: My son and daughter never help pick up the rooms. This morning I even got stuck to a wad of gum when I sat down.

A: That was no big deal. All you had to do was nicely but firmly asking them to remove it for you.

B: I freaked out! Teens today really need to shape up!

A: But do you know kids today are also the unhappiest? The number of muggings and rapes is appalling; their confusion about the future is mind-boggling; and all the temptations from friends and mass media are horrendous! In our days the only problem we had to face was poverty.

B: What temptations?

A: Drugs, sex, brand names, fancy cell phones, and the list goes on. All those make them disoriented.

B: Right. Some even thus went for prostituting or trafficking in narcotics.

A: They surely need help, and we parents and teachers mustn't shirk our responsibility.

B: But they are so perverse and unable to cope!

A: Just remember that those fledgling teens are also vulnerable, maladjusted, helpless, anxious, and even depressed. Some even suffer from insomnia!

B:　What should I do then?

A:　First you need to accept them with great empathy then seek wisdom from books or experts.　Just for your reference, I always adopt the carrot-and-stick strategy, which works well!

48. You Can Run the Show, Too!

A: How can I become a great teacher?

B: You'll need great technique, content and presentation! A good teacher also exudes passion for teaching and captures students' attention by well-prepared teaching plans.

A: I already am doing my best. But it's just frustrating on seeing some students looking bored in class!

B: A nice teacher always produces an optimal classroom climate and links the subject of whatever he/she teaches to everyday life and to students' future career.

A: I still don't know what to do with those who are simply detestable!

B: Seek out! Discover their merits and talents. Never give up on them! Every single one of them has some kind of potential.

A: It's hard. Sometimes I just can't run the show.

B: Yes, you can --- if you are truly competent, uncompromisingly strict, and almost always forgiving.

A: I favor those who look neat and behave well.

B: Don't do that. Some students are just victimized by their family backgrounds. If we don't accept and help them, who will? NEVER PLAY FAVORITES!

49. Rise above It!

A: I feel fidgety.

B: A penny for your thoughts!

A: My hands are tied because I haven't had a raise for five years.　I might as well start getting in with my superiors!

B: You don't go to all lengths for getting promoted, okay?　Money naturally comes as the result of success.

A: But I'm already working around the clock!

B: Lots of very hard workers haven't been very successful, even though I do believe in the virtue of diligence.

A: You're being contradictory here.

B: You'll need more to succeed, such as absolute optimism, keen insights, vivid creativity, harmonious interpersonal relationships and a good health.

A: Then I can expect a carefree life when I succeed?

B: Not at all!　Success without happiness is emptiness.

A: Gosh, you're testy.　What are you trying to get at?

B: We'll come to that later.

50. Exuding Personal Magnetism

A: I wish to become a real beauty.

B: We all do!　But you'll need to possess both inner beauty and external beauty.

A: I know that external beauty is having a pretty face and outer appearance.

B: It includes our signature style of clothing, face, figure, hair, etiquette (which includes manners, poise and hygiene), walking techniques, sitting techniques, facial expressions, voice production and even public speaking!

A: Imagine!

B: Nonetheless, while all these things are important, they are not primary.

A: Are you kidding me?　What's missing there?

B: You're not beautiful on the outside until you possess your beauty on the inside. It's inner beauty that helps you exude personal magnetism for long.

A: How can I obtain inner beauty then?

B: It's a state of mind, and you need to cultivate your lifestyle with it.　These inner qualities are quietly translated into outward visual beauty.

A: I don't understand.

B: It's about the love and self-discipline you have in you.

A: Are you talking about altruism?

B: Indeed!　Unselfish love makes you cheerful, forgiving, caring, understanding and humble.

A: It's so cool!　And self-discipline makes me beautiful, too?

B: Definitely!　Self-discipline makes you staid, trustworthy, self-confident and respectable.

A: I doubt if I can do them all!

B: But those together compose the real charm.　Charm is an intangible and magical quality that makes you truly beautiful!

51. Urban Space

A: Have you noticed that we city people are living in decreasing spaces?

B: Yes, owing to the intense urbanization.

A: But cities must grow in order to retain their economic, cultural, social, entertaining and intellectual vitality!

B: Exactly.   And parking has become a pain in the neck!

A: I agree with you.   Our government and private entrepreneurs should come up with some immediate and innovative solutions to counter the space problem.

B: Especially in central business districts where growth is most stifled!   Last time it took me more than an hour to find parking space in downtown Taipei! Imagine!

A: Without sufficient space, the rebirth and the rehabilitation of the city cannot proceed.

B: Consequently, its dynamic socioeconomic mechanism cannot function!

A: You've hit the bull's eye!

52. Icebergs (I)

A: I dreamed of icebergs last night.　Have you ever seen icebergs?

B: Twice.

A: I have only seen them on *Discovery* Channel!　They were magnificent!

B: They are!

A: Why are icebergs white?　Are there some materials in it?

B: No, the white color comes from the tiny air bubbles in the ice; and they have a blue tint when they are bubble free.

A: Where does the blue come from?

B: Same as the light phenomimen that tints the sky.　Once in Alaska I even saw an icerbeg glowing in sapphire blue!

A: Why do I feel so left in the dust?　I should travel more often to broaden my horizons!

B: You should, but no hurry.　When it's time, it's time.

A: I see. But how do icebergs form?

B: They actually come from glaciers.

A: Glaciers?　What do glaciers have to do with icebergs?

B: We'll come to that later.

53. Icebergs (II)

A: Glaciers come from snow. They are actually a result of an acculation of snow over thousands of years!

B: And they break up into icebergs?

A: Close. They creep under their own weight and the edge breaks off when it advances into the sea. That's iceberg!

B: We often hear the "tip of an iceberg." How much of an icerberg is below water?

A: The density of ice, 900kg per cubic meter, is lower than that of sea seater, which is 1025kg per cubic meter. The ratio of these densities, 900:1025, equivelant to 9:10, makes 9/10 of the iceberg's mass below water.

B: Wow! So the tip of an iceberg is only 1/10 of the whole thing?

A: That's right. But do you know that icebergs are often stuck on the seabed instead of floating around?

B: That's amazing!

A: I have a question for you: Are icebergs salty?

B: Let's see.

A: May I remind you that they come from snow, not sea water?

B: I got it! They are edible!

54. Typhoons, Floods and Mudslides

Being an island located in semi-tropical area, Taiwan suffers a lot from typhoons. Typhoon is a tropical cyclone which is a storm that derives its energy from cloud formation and rainfall. This is unlike mid-latitude storms that derive their power from a temperature gradient (cold front).

Typhoons often hit Taiwan, causing floods, mudslides, landslides, etc., resulting in loss of human life and property. Recently a typhoon has pounded northern and central Taiwan, and local media reports say some 4,000 residents have been trapped in Hsyinyi village in the county of Nantou after bridges were destroyed and homes buried.

As Taipei city braces for the typhoon, the authorities have shut down financial markets, schools and offices. The weather has caused major disruption to the island's transport network. International flights are carrying on as normal but all domestic flights have been suspended after a Far Eastern Air Transport aircraft skidded off the runway when it landed in Taipei earlier in the day. In addition, railway services linking Taipei and eastern coastal cities have also been suspended.

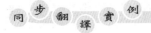

55. The Greenhouse Effect On Earth (I)

A: The greenhouse effect is being discussed by people. What is it anyway? I know what a greenhouse is for plants, but what does it have to do with the earth?

B: Because the earth's atmosphere warms our planet in the same way as an ordianary greenhouse is warmed. Our greenhouse is made of glass, which lets in light while preventing heat from escaping. Similarly, the gases in the atmosphere function like the glass of a greenhouse!

A: What gases?

B: Carbon dioxide, nitrous oxide, methane, etc. appear transparent to certain wavelengths of the sun's radiance.

A: Got it! These transparent gases allow the sun's radiant energy to penetrate into our atmosphere and reach the earth! But there are clouds to block the energy!

B: Exactly! But clouds, particles in the air and ice caps also reflect only 30% of this radiation. But this isn't totally bad! If this natural barrier weren't there, the heat would escape into space, making the mean global temperature as low as –18 Celsius.

A: What's the mean temperature now?

B: We'll come to that later.

56. The Greenhouse Effect On Earth (II)

A: You were mentioning the mean global temperature.

B: Right, thanks for reminding me. The current mean global temperature is 15 Celsius.

A: My goodness. Which means without these gases the mean temperature could be as much as 33 degrees lower!

A: How's that calculated?

B: −18 degrees as opposed to 15.

A: Right. Nonetheless, some scientists are concerned that we are producing too many greenhouse gases, which may warm this planet too much.

A: Again, that's another side effect of civilization.

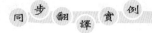

57. Air Pollution

A: The sky looks hazy!

B: Because the air is heavily polluted.   Factories and automobiles are all emitting chemicals and toxic gases.

A: What are the main air pollutants?

B: Two of them are carbon monoxide, which is odorless, and nitrogen dioxide, which smells bad.

A: Where do they come from?

B: They both come from burning fossil fuels, such as gasoline.

A: Are there other pollutants?

B: Some particulate matters, which is unwanted solid or liquid matter, lead, etc. These are all poisonous to our air.

A: Do they make skies hazy?

B: They are most visible in big cities like Beijing, Shanghai, Taipei, etc.   Quite a few cities are suffering from bad environmental problems caused by the drastic growth rates in the population and in the economy.

58. The Ozone Layer

A: I've often heard the term as "the ozone layer." Why are scientists so bothered about this?

B: Because ozone acts like a sunblock which filters out the ultra-violet rays from the sun, but it is wearing off!

A: Well, I wear sunblock in order not to get tanned, and more importantly, I don't want my skin to age rapidly.

B: Yes, primarily. The thinning ozone layer is making us exposed to excessive UV light, which not only makes our skin age, but might cause skin cancer. Seniors especially must protect their skin from the sun damage that can lead to wrinkles, actinic keratoses and cancer.

A: What about the dark pigments? I've heard that Asians get less damaged from the sun because we have more dark pigments than Caucasions?

B: You mean "melanin" ? We indeed are luckier than Caucasians because we have enough melanin in skin to resist photo aging, but sunscreen protection is still highly recommended by dermatologists. Especially those who have pale skin, which is the most susceptible to sun damage.

59. Teenagers, Parents and Schools

A: I don't get it.   By the time when teengagers are in senior high, they should have already spent at least 15 years negotiating with their parents. But why is it also the exact time for them to be confused and most rebellious?

B: Parents, society and schools should all be responsible for this, especially the parents!

A: Teenagers today seem to be well informed but lack judgment; they dwell in the global village but lack perception; they are passionate while having low EQ and AQ.

B: I know EQ is short for Emotion Quotient. What is AQ?

A: Adversity Quotient.

B. That's important, too. Parents can't just attribute their children's behavior and performance to schools.

A: I agree.   There are no problem children, only problem parents.   Children look at them as the best role models since babyhood.

B: Taking going to college for example, independent and comfident students make clear decisions with their self-analyses and with the information available about going to on to university.   But those aren't the majority. Most kids are still confused.

A: Just to be fair, not all parents know how to help their children.　I personally think that teachers can reach out to increase families' involvement.

B: What do you suggest?

A: Junior and senior high schools should not only communite with all families, but conduct various activities that involve families in teenagers' development, romances, learning, and choosing what to study for the future.

60. US - China -Taiwan Relations

A: Do you think the United States will defend Taiwan if it is under attack?

B: Have you noticed that America reaffirms her backing for the One-China policy?

A: What's One-China policy?

B: It recognizes Taiwan as part of China and that America is non-supportive for Taiwan independence or Taiwan's any actions to change the status quo.

A: Why's that?

B: The US does not wish to see Taiwan and China reunified and grow into a giant, and she has long created a positive image of US-China relations because China is an important power in Asia, occupying a critical strategic position globally.

A: The States also needs Taiwan to buy weapons from her.

B: Meanwhile, she needs China to be her key partner to solve the North Korea issue.

A: So she cannot offend China.

B: Nope.　But China currently is facing lots of problems including at least religious freedom, weapons proliferation issues raised by the States, human rights and economic growth.

61. Taiwan (I)—Its History

A: Why is Taiwan also named "Formosa"?

B: It means "lovely" and was named by Portugese when they took up Taiwan.

A: Really? That's cute.

B: But I don't think Taiwan has a history complimenting this adorable name.

A: Why's that? Does Taiwan have a miserable story?

B: After Jia Wu War in 1895, *the Treaty of Shimonoseki* forced China to cede Taiwan to Japan, and Taiwan suffered a lot under the Japanese control.

A: No wonder the mother of a friend of mine still speaks Japanese. But I thought Taiwan reverted to China after WWII.

B: It did. Then two million Nationalists fled to Taiwan when they were defeated by Communit Chinese.

A: And there came the 228 Incident of Taiwan?

B: Yes, in 1947. During which lots of people, including Taiwanese and so-called Mainland Chinese were killed.

A: Think on the bright side. In the following 50 some years, the government gradually democratized Taiwan and incorporated all the people.

B: As a matter of fact, Taiwan started experiencing democracy under Late President Chiang Ching-kuo's guidance. Taiwan even prospered and became one of East Asia's "four economic tigers."

A: And Taiwan even underwent its first transfer of power in 2000 from the KMT to the DPP!

B: It surely did!

62. Taiwan (II)— Its Politics

A: How many political parties are formed in Taiwan?

B: Currently there are five major parties: DPP, KMT, PFP, TSU, and CNP.

A: Among which, DPP and TSU oppose the stand that Taiwan will reunify with Mainland China.

B: And those who are against Taiwan independence advocate a gradual reunification with China through peace for another 50 years in order not to turn Taiwan into a battlefield.

A: Taiwan's international relationships seem quite complex. For example, Paracel Islands are under China, whereas claimed by Taiwan; Senkaku Islands (Diaoyu Tai) is administered by Japan, whereas also claimed by Taiwan.

B: Right. Media coverage and protest actions are making these issues conspicuous.

63. How Arabs See America (I) (The Cons)

A: I really sympathize with Iraq.   Two major Western powers have turned it into a battlefield.

B: Its people suffer a lot.   As a matter of fact, Arabs want nothing but a better life in the Middle East.

A: The only power that can end their religious and ethnic conflicts is America.   But this "world cop" has caused more bloodshedding in the Middle East.

B: I once heard on news that Arabs would all be happy if the United States really spoke of regional disarmanent and stability in the Gulf region. But they have been compelled to feel desperate, disappointed and irritated.

A: I don't blame them. They feel that the US seems to have always been more interested in their oil than their wellbeing.

B: And now the anti-Americanism is widely across the Middle East.

A: Especially among the Islamic fundamentalists.   Once in the largest mosque in Iraq a prominent Islamic cleric once told his followers during a surmon that America is after two things: Oil and helping Israel for her own benefit.

64. How Arabs See America (II) (The Pros)

A: Meanwhile, there is a muted minority in the Arab world who are sympathetic with America.

B: What's their viewpoint?

A: They thank America for her courage and justice of playing the role as the world's super cop while the whole world is adopting nonintervetion in other countries' internal matters.

B: So they expect that US and Britain will protect international peace and norms?

A: They do.　They also praise America for having intervened in Afghanistan against Taliban regime.　They claim that the Muslim world is too weak and chaotic to maintain its own peace and order, so they might as well leave it to the world leader.

B: But a significant fact is that the pros and cons unanimously expect peaceful diplomatic means, such as negotiations with America's help.

A: But America and Britain took on new enemies by shelling, making people like Osama Bin Laden rise.

B: Bin Laden can always recruit new followers.

A: All and all, I would say that the Arab world is eager to see a fair policy of disarmanent in that area.

B: And that includes Israel.

65. Al Jazeera

A: Have you heard of Al Jazeera?

B: Yup.　A very famous television network in Middle East. It has broadcast videotapes of how Iraqi war prisoners were tortured by American and British soldiers and the process of how an American hostage was beheaded by their militants. What about it?

A: Well, their branch office in Baghdad has been ordered to close by the prime Minister of Iraq.

B: Really?　But Al Jazeera broadcasts to millions of Arab viewers and is the only TV network providing coverage from areas thought to be dangerous for Western reporters. Why was it shut?

A: Well, the new Iraqi government said Al Jazeera disturbs the secutiry in Iraq and has to be temporarily closed.

B: What a pity! It's the primary source of news from Iraq! The closing is contrary to the new government's pledge as to start a brand new area of free speech and openness.

A: It has long been criticized as encouraging militants and biased against America.

66. US vs. NK (US Stance)

A:　How come all those years' talks and negotiations between US and North Korea haven't reached any results yet?

B:　Because there are fundamental differences between their positions.

A:　I know America has long insisted that North Korea immediately dismantle its nuclear weapons.

B:　Right, and in a thorough, non-negotiagle, verifiable and irreversible way.

A:　But why would North Korea do it?　Are they receiving any beneficial proposals from the States?

B:　So far the US has not yet submited any concrete propals, but emphasizes that North Korea must abandon all its nuclear programs.　In addtion, conventional forces, biochemical weapons, human rights and numerous other issues should also be reevaluated and properly adjusted.

A:　America is trying hard to maintain peace in Asia.

B:　In a way, yes.　But a strong nuke country in Asia conflicts the American interest as far as her global strategy is concerned.

67. NK vs. US (NK's Stance)

A: How has North Korea reacted so far toward America's request?

B: It certainly isn't happy about America's high profile on completely eliminating its nuclear derrant force. But it responds that the solution can be properly achieved with a fair and flexible proposal.

A: To meet mutual interests?

B: Exactly. It will freeze only its nuclear weapon programs while exempting those for peaceful use, and it demands that the US should do something in return.

A: That makes sence. What do they request?

B: That America should remove it from the blacklist of those who sponsor terrorism, provide oil and electricity, and lift the political and economic sanctions and blockades on it.

A: But I thought North Korea denied its unarium based nuclear programs?

B: It did, saying that America was making a groundless accusation; but it finally admitted in 2005 that they did possess nuclear weapons.

68. About Russia—A "Welfare" Policy

A: President Vladimir Pudin promised that a major goal of his second term is improving living standards for millions of impoverished Russians. Has his promise been fulfilled?

B: What should I say? Russia's upper house of parliament approves a social reform bill which has been criticized as accomplishing the opposite.

A: What's included in the bill?

B: That the government is going to end free transportation and medicine provided for the elderly, disabled, etc.

A: Why did the parliament pass such a bill?

B: It's said to be the rubber stamp for the Kremlin. Among 179 seats 156 approved with one abstention.

A: Why would the government eliminate benefits that Russia's most vulnerable people have long relied on since Soviet era?

B: You tell me! But I do know that some young protesters staged a huger strike.

A: The poor, the disabled, the elderly and WWII veterans will be profoundly affected, but they can only be subjugated by politicians.

69. Major Economic Policies on Mainland China (I)

A: After the bamboo curtain was lifted, China has become the largest developing country in the world.

B: Exactly. And the PRC government has accumulated certain experiences coping with various complicated situations since reform and opening up.

A: Her land, resources and huge population all suggest that she has a tremendous potential development.

B: You've said it! Imagine what a huge market that 1.3 billion people can provide?

A: With her low labor cost, hard work and intelligent people, China is doing an amazing job on processing industries. So I believe the global processing industries will eventually be transferred to China.

B: Do you think China can successfully accommodate long-term economic growth? Can she develop from labor-intensive to capital and technology intensive?

A: I wouldn't doubt that. Her several breakthroughs will make her economic transformation irresistible.

B: What breakthroughs?

A: I will tell you later.

70. Major Economic Policies on Mainland China (II)

A: I know that fundamental changes must take place in the institutional mechanism, especially within the government.

B: You're right. PRC has relaxed governmental control, added with generously encouraging both domestic and international investments by improving financing, transportation, and legal environment, etc.

A: What about the state-owned enterprises? These used to monopolize the market.

B: Not any more. These enterpreses are swifting their focus on assisting all forms of ownerships in the country.

A: You're saying that China is pursuing development without reserve?

B: I wouldn't say so. But I would say that she is seeking from A to Z development which is well coordinated and sustainable.

A: I believe this new concept has replaced the old one which pursued merely the growth of GDP.

71. An Appreciation of Renminbi Yuan

A: Did you know that the Renminbi yuan appreciated by 2.1% last night?

B: Yes, it was quite sudden after Beijing has long resisted pressure to revaluate it!

A: But this isn't the first revelation of this currency. It appreciated by 18.5% against the US dollar between 1994 and 2002.

B: Was Renminbi ever devalued in history?

A: Yes. In 1994 it depreciated against the US dollar by half its 1986 rate. Then it went up as the Chinese economy began to boom. It has been like a roller coaster!

B: Do you think the rate will keep climbing?

A: I guess so because the 2.1% is only the initial upward adjustment. China has decided to adopt a "managed floating" policy based on an unspecified basket of currencies.   In other words, the exchange rate will be market-oriented.

B: You're saying the exchange rate will be more flexible?   Then I guess I can expect some further gains!

72. Zhejiang—One of the Richest Provinces in China

A: My husband has just been promoted, but he will also be transferred to their Zhejiang branch office in China.

B: Zhejiang? That's a nice place. I've read from the newspaper that it occupies more than half of the total import and export in China. That's an extremely prosperous province!

A: But that's not my concern. I'm more concerned with my children's education.

B: That'll be the last thing you should worry about. There are quite reputable schools in this province, ranging from elementarty schools to universities. Besides, nothing is more important than a family being together.

A: Why is Zhejiang growing so rapidly? It was still quite underdeveoped last time when I travelled there.

B: It's all owing to their "going global" policy, which integrates and accomodates different types of ownerships at the core of policy making.

A: Wow, "going global" compared with the "localization" in Taiwan …

B: The consequences are self-explanatory.

73. Taiwanese Investments in China

A: The number of applications for investing on China is climbing up!

B: This year nearly 1,400 registered between January and July, which is approximately 21% higher than the number for the same period last year.

A: What's the total amount of investments for this time slot?

B: The approved amount alone totalled US$3.8 billion, practically 50% higher than last year.

A: Wow! Fifty percent is a lot! Where and on what does the investment go?

B: The investment goes mainly in Shanghai, Guandong and Zhejiang for electronic and electrical appliance manufacturing, basic medical manufacturing, plastic manufactung, chemical production and vehicle manufacturing.

A: I've heard that many US Internet companies have entered China, too?

B: Yes, through merges and acquisitions.

74. Singapore — A Quick Look

A: Why do most Singaporans speak English?

B: Because Singapore was first founded as a British trading colony as early as 1819.

A: Is it still a colony of Britain?

B: Not after 1963 when it joined the Malaysian Federation.

A: That explains why its ethnic groups include Malay.

B: Exactly.   Even today you can hear Malay spoken across this country.

A: But Singapore is an independent state country now.

B: A state country?   It must be relatively small?

A: Quite!   Its area totals 693 km², now you compare that with the area of Taiwan which is 36,000 km².

B: But its historical background as an ex-British trading colony and wise leadership have made it one of the world's most prosperous countries.

A: Indeed.   Its port tops the busiest in the world in terms of tonnage handled.

B: And this state country's per capital GDP is as high as that of the leading countries in Western Europe!

A: That's remarkable!   Strong international trading links, wise and flexible diplomatic strategies and diligent people have all contributed to their prosperity.

B: Unfortunately, it unavoidably suffers from industrial pollution, and its limited land availability has produced great waste disposal problems as well.

A: Ya, I know. It once even had smoke and haze resulting from forest fires in Indonesia.

75. The Depreciation Of the American Dollar

A: Gosh, the American dollar has dropped nearly 30% with the past 10 years!

B: That's a strategy.

A: What do you mean? Isn't a strong currency equivalent to a strong national purchasing power?

B: Not necessarily. High dollar value not only prices exports out of world market, but also depresses the profits for multinational conglomerates.

A: Don't get it.

B: Profits made abroad come in local currencies, right?

A: Right.

B: Take American transnational conglomerates for example, do they prefer to have local currencies translated into higher or lower figures in dollar terms?

A: I got it. The strong US dollar is cutting their profits!

B: There you go. Meanwhile, the US needs a high inflow in foreign capital to finance her balance of payments dificit, which means a weak dollar policy would be beneficial to the US economy.

A: You are good!

76. World Economy

A: Have you noticed a slowdown in world economy in past five years?

B: I surely have.   It's mainly caused by the slowdown in PPP.

A: That rings a bell to me.   What's that?

B: Purshicasing Power Parity, remember? And the U.S. China, India and Japan are the top four economics in this respect.

A: This economoic recession has forced numerous highly leveraged consumers into bankruptcies.

B: Fortunately, Americans on average remain in shape, thanks to the stock market boom during 1990s.

A: How's the world's employment market?

B: It's doing better than earlier expected, showing some pick up since 2000.

A: But I know that a significant number run into debt, borrowing more than they can pay back.

77. Japan—The Bubble Economy

A: You can see Japanese tourists all around the world.

B: I used to.　Unfortunately, the number is decreasing.

A: What happened?

B: The bubble economy collapsed.

A: What's bubble economy?

B: It's a vicious circle. When speculation in a commodity causes a boost of the price, more speculation is produced. In no time the price becomes so rediculous that it drops as suddenly as a drop of water falls down.

A: You mean like a crash?

B: It is a crash!　As a matter of fact, Japanese economists have recently warned that the total amount of Japan's bad bank loans is almost equivalent to half of its GDP.

A: Wow! That's bad!

B: Japan's industrialized, free-market economy used to rank the third largest in the world after the United States and China in terms of PPP.

A: What's PPP?

B: Purchasing Power Parity.　And now it falls to the fourth largest in the world after the United States, China and recently India. And the stagnation is actually

creating more bad loans which grow as fast as the old debts are being paid off!

A: Aren't there counter-policies for this crisis?

B: There are.　But the US dollar policy jeopardizes its economy.

A: How come?

B: Because the depreciating US dollar conflicts with the Japanese Yen. Same as America, Japan also needs a falling yen to boost its economy!

A: So Japan is now at the end of its rope?

B: As far as I know, it now relies a lot on its Fiscal System Council.

A: Is that a government agency? What does it do?

B: It's under the Ministry of Finance, composed of business executives, entrepreneus, scholars and even journalists for discussing critical topics related to the country's budget, settlement, and the accounting.

A: And these experts research and solve those economic problems?

B: They conduct very in-depth research from expenditure cuts to locating an appropriate level of debt-to-GDP ratio.

78. Petroleum

A: Oil is the most important commodity in the world, and such high energy costs are derailing the world economy. Did you know that a $15 per barrel rise will add 1% to unemployment in the States?

B: Really? Why isn't enough oil being pumped to meet world demand for reducing prices to a sustainable level?

A: Because the once-mighty OPEC (The Organization of Petroleum Exporting Countries) is ebbing away since its member countries control less share of the world's total oil supplies than previously.

B: How's that?

A: Because several non-OPEC countries have ramped up production.

B: Who are they?

A: Russia, Norway and Mexico; and new flows of oil fields have been discovered in Africa and South America.

B: With so much oil in the world, why is the price is still so high?

A: Because only the OPEC is playing the game by the rule. However, currently only three OPEC members are in the world's top-10 oil producers — these three alone provide more than half of the world's crude oil exports.

B: this high percentage should entitle them to speak aloud!

A: The Western powers in the Middle East, especially the recent war in Iraq have caused immense disruption of oil exports in the Middle East.

B: The prices of transportations, materials, real estates, cosmetics, etc. are all profoundly and immediately affected!

A: Petroleum prices matter enormously for everyone's daily life.

79. Qingming Shang He Tu (Along the River during the Ching-Ming Festival)

A: Have you seen a hand scroll painting at Shih-lin National Palace Museum, named "Along the River during the Ching-Ming Festival?"

B: I have, it's a long hand scroll format, and I even bought a silk fan with its image on. It looks quite exquisite.

A: It portrays the unique lifestyle and customs of the Ming and Ching dynasties.

B: I have found women washing clothes, a monkey show and acrobats performing along the river.

A: There are also kids playing, a theatrical performance, and many other forms of entertainment.

B: I like its brilliant colors and fine brushwork.

A: That's a characteristic of Ching's court painting, which reflects Western painting techniques.

80. The Jadeite Cabbage

A: Let me look at your jade bangle.   It's so pretty!

B: Thank you.   So is your pendant.   Jade is believed by Chinese people to be an auspicious material.

A: But jade carving is hard, which often requires a considerable amount of experience and effort!

B: Right.   You'll have to suit the features to the material.   For example, the jadeite cabbage found in Empress Ci-xi's tomb is a jade carving in white and green with two delicate green grasshoppers, and its lifelikeness fascinates everyone.

A: Why are grasshoppers carved on it? Do they symbolize anything?

B: Grasshoppers in ancient China symbolized great fertility.   In the ancient Chinese agricultural society manpower was needed to do the farming and fertility was considered a blessing.   The grasshoppers, resting on the pure white and green jade, meant a clean family would have plentiful offspring.

A: Cool! One piece of jade presents that much culture, heh?

81. Patents

A:　I'm going to file a patent application for my new invention.

B:　Why?　Are you going to mass-produce it?

A:　I might.　So I want to protect my right of the invention.

B:　Yes. It's miserable that someone's lifelong effort on inventing a new product is devastated by very rapid and massive pirating in the market.

A:　My invention is small compared with many others into which much time, money, effort on research and experiments may put.

B:　No wonder the patent law is needed.　If the achievements of the research can't be protected, who will invest on all the stuff again?

A:　According to the patent law, the patentee has the right to exclude people for pirating, making, selling, using and importing the product or method associated with the invention.

B:　Which means the patent right is an exclusive right! But what if two people apply for the same invention at the same time?

A:　Here then comes the "first filing principle." No matter what the inventions' priority is, only the first applicant will get the patent right, if there are two or more applicant who have the same invention.

82. Court Interpretation & Vocabulary

This defendant has been indicted by the prosecutor for the charge of unaccomplished homicide. The defendant argued that it was an accident and claimed that he'll accuse the plaintiff of slander instead.

The plaintiff's lawyer claimed that the defendant intended to kill his wife quite a few times. The first time he tried to burn her with gasoline, the victim escaped; the second time he used a venomous snake, which didn't work out either. The third time he stabbed her. That was it! She finally called the police.

According to the prosecutor's investigation, the defendant had extramarital relations and even got remarried behind the victim's back. He was caught and sentenced by court to have committed the crime of bigamy. The home wrecker was sentenced guilty as offending family.

After listening to the defendant's defense, rejoinder and rebuttal, the judge reprimanded the defendant's sophistry, distortion and cruelty, convicted him of concurrence criminality of arson, bigamy and attempted homicide and sentenced him to life imprisonment with no chance of parole.

83. A Model Court

A: I hate going to courts. They don't treat people with respect.

B: That's why I was impressed with the L.A. High Court where fairness, accessibility, integrity and responsiveness & responsibility were given to court participants.

A: I can imagine what "fair", "responsiveness & responsibility" imply. But what are involved in accessibility and integrity?

B: "Accessibility", according to the court, aims at helping people identify and remove barriers to access all legal matters. And "integrity", from what the court explains, includes protecting individual rights, liberties, confidentiality and developing employees who conduct themselves ethically and professionally.

A: Wow! The L.A. High court should be an excellent role model for all the courts on earth.

84. Applying for a US Student Visa

A: I plan to study in the States next fall. What kind of visa should I apply for?

B: Either the F-1 or M-1 if you meet the criteria.

A: What's F-1?

B: The F visa is for nonimmigrants who wish to study — F-1 for you and F-2 for your dependents.

A: And the M visa?

B: It's reserved for those who wish to attend nonacademic courses.

A: I see. And what do they require?

B: The I-20, showing you are approved to enroll in either an academic program, a language program, or a vocational program.

A: Where do I get the I-20?

B: The school will send it to you by mail. But the school must be approved by the USCIS.

A: What's USCIS?

B: U-S-C-I-S, representing US citizenship and Immigration Services.

A: Do I need to take TOEFL or a similar exam to prove my English proficiency?

B: Not necessarily, but that'll be required by the school. For obtaining a student visa, you must either be proficient in English or be enrolled in English language courses.

A: What else do I need?

B: You will also show them sufficient funds for supporting your entire process of studying there, including the tuition, living expenses, insurance, etc.

A: Is it hard to get a student visa?

B: Not at all.　Just prepare the money, your English proficiency, the I-20 form, and relax. They welcome nice foreign students, ok?

85. Obtaining a US Work Permit

A: I might try to find a moonlighting when I study in the States.

B: You will want to apply for an EAD unless you are a citizen or a lawful resident.

A: What's EAD?

B: It's Employment Authorization Document issued by USCIS, which allows you to work in the States.

A: How can I get one?

B: Go visit their website, and remember to apply for a renewal six months before the original one expires.

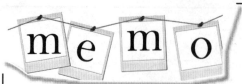